confessions of a

SERIAL
EGG
DONOR

JULIA DEREK

ADRENALINE BOOKS

ISBN 0-9749079-0-1

LCCN 2004103902

ATTENTION CORPORATIONS, UNIVERSITIES, COLLEGES, AND PROFESSIONAL ORGANIZATIONS: Quantity discounts are available on bulk purchases of this book for educational, gift purposes, or as premiums for increasing magazine subscriptions or renewals. Special books or book excerpts can also be created to fit specific needs. For more information, contact Adrenaline Books at (646) 425-9000.

*For all the young women
who make children possible for others
by donating their eggs*

CONTENTS

PROLOGUE

The tears have been coming for hours now. Like on so many other days, they just keep on coming and coming. It is a mad stream of annoying wetness. I'm sure they will continue forever, that no part of this lunacy will ever stop. I want to scream out loud. Or kick the wall if I thought it would help. Pull my hair out. But none of it works. I know because I have tried all three.

How did I end up like this? This was not the way I had planned it. Or at least, this is not what I had expected would happen. Not even in my wildest dreams did I ever think I would find myself in this state, lying in bed for days and days, unable to move, my insides drying out, my head aching with such brutality that something up there must have broken. I, the invincible; I, Superwoman; I, the person who was naturally immune against any diseases or physical aches, who thought people were wimps when they took a week off work because they had caught the flu, who once couldn't remember for sure whether PMS was the abbreviation of one of those so-called women's ailments or if it was really a new rap artist.

It seems as if the despair won't ever go away, that it will only grow and grow until there is nothing else left and it has taken over my entire being. This despair is enormously big and dark, yet shrinking smaller and smaller, making it hard for me to breathe. It is as if somebody has pulled a trash bag over my head and is closing it tightly around my neck. It is so unbearable that some days I find myself begging to die, I find myself praying to whomever is in charge of those kinds of things, this somebody or something who apparently isn't planning to make whatever the fuck is happening to me stop, *to please let me die. Anything but*

1

this, anything but another minute of having to live in this hell.

Of course, the worst part of all of this is the feeling that I'm going insane. Completely nuts, loony bin caliber crazy. And every week this feeling is getting worse. It certainly looks like I'm losing it to the people around me. I don't blame them. I really don't... But, you see, I know I'm not going crazy. The one thing that keeps me from going truly crazy is this very knowledge, the knowledge that it is something else that's making me feel all these huge, horrible feelings; it is something else that's making me lose all control. I know there is a single and definite reason for why this is happening to me – and that I'm not it.

She has tried to convince me otherwise. In her Southern drawl, poking away at my insecurities like a defense lawyer pokes away at the plaintiff's character before a jury, she told me, "You know why this is happening, Julia, you know what I'm talking about. Everything in your life is not the way it should be. You know what I mean. You have some problems. And that's why you feel this way."

I couldn't believe what she was saying. She was actually trying to make me think that this monster about to take me over so completely was created by me, and me alone. It was only when she had said this that I realized that she was right, that I indeed had a problem. One very serious problem.

She was not going to do what had to be done for me to get out of this.

AND SO IT BEGAN

read the ad in the paper before me once more: "*Egg Donor Wanted. Infertile couple searching for tall (5'8"minimum), athletic, green eyes, brunette egg donor between the ages of 18-30. Preferably from Northern or Eastern Europe. Very discreet. Compensation:* **$3,500.** *Call 567-XXXX.*"

What was this? Egg donor...? Did this mean what I thought it did? Did women who couldn't have their own kids really *pay money* to other women in exchange for their eggs? Did that really *work...*? Well, it must because why else would someone advertise for it. How weird... Or then again, maybe it wasn't, considering that men could be sperm donors. Hmmm... OK, let's see here: A woman might actually be able to get 3,500 dollars for one of her eggs? This just sounded too good to be true... I leaned back in the leather chair I had been sitting in for the last two hours going over the classifieds in today's *Washington Post*. With that amount, all my problems would be taken care of... I was filled with a strong feeling that this might indeed be the answer.

I had been in Washington D.C. studying journalism for a little more than three months when last night, finally, the bitter truth came crashing down on me: If I didn't find a way to make more money soon, I could look forward to sitting on a plane back home to Sweden before even starting my next semester in January. What was left of my savings wouldn't last much longer; at the most, two more months. My eyes had stung from hot tears at the thought of having to leave America, this country I had come to love even deeper than what I had thought I would. Ever since I was a kid I had fantasized about living here – and now I was! I think I had always known in my heart that where I was born wasn't really meant for me; I needed something much bigger, much more diverse, a country with the power to let you be you, to be truly happy. I loved the challenges America promised, challenges that were impossible to find in a place as sheltered as Sweden. I loved the self-confident, go-getting spirit of its people and I couldn't get enough of their enthusiasm and courtesy. (In Sweden, modesty is king, as well as a reserved, to the point of nearly brusque demeanor.) From the very day back in August when I arrived here I felt as if that what people always say about America, that you can do anything here, was really true. No, going back just wasn't an option. I couldn't bear the thought of it.

As it happened, I did fit the description of the person they were advertising for almost perfectly. I was five feet eight inches tall; I was twenty-four years old; ever since I became a teenager people kept telling me how athletic I looked (which I had always found extremely insulting); my hair was somewhere between dirty blonde and light brown; I most certainly had green eyes, and even though I was only Northern-European by passport, not by ancestry, I still qualified since my mother was from the Ukraine – definitely Eastern Europe – and my father from the country formerly known as Yugoslavia (which is more *South*-Eastern Europe, but I figured it was close enough). So I should give them a call then…

Before my famous nerves got a chance to make themselves noticed – I happen to be one of those people who possess a close to compulsive fear of calling up strangers – I grabbed the cordless phone that rested next to the newspaper and punched in the number in the ad.

But as I brought the phone to my ear, the obvious suddenly struck me: If I donated my eggs to a woman – or sold actually – I would become the mother to that woman's child, wouldn't I? Yes, of course I would…

I wasn't sure how I felt about *that* notion. Rapidly, I ended the call and let the phone drop into my lap. Hmmm… Maybe this wasn't such a great idea after all…

I switched on the TV and began to restlessly skip from one channel to another. If only I had a green card! Once more I contemplated the thought of begging the organizers of the one-of-a-kind international program I and fifty other Swedes had crossed the Atlantic to study under to help find me a job on campus. And again I discarded it; I hadn't yet reached the point where I could bear the embarrassment that would entail. Also, it wasn't likely to succeed anyway, as we weren't really allowed to work at George Mason, the campus where our course took place; the organizers merely rented space there for the classes. This policy had been made abundantly clear to all the students long before our departure upon which we had been made to prove that we had enough money to live on while in America for the nine months the program lasted. The financial aid the Swedish government awarded us only covered tuition and housing. By promising them that my mother would give me an additional 1,200 dollars in January – the amount I had in my bank account at the time – they let me go.

Of course, this promise had been a white lie; my factory-working mother barely had money to cover her own expenses. Instead, I had counted on getting a few jobs teaching aerobics with the help of my recently acquired teaching certification. Well aware that gyms just like restaurants didn't always care about their employees having valid work papers, I figured it would be a matter of a week or two before that happened. And then I would be set.

However, I learned quickly that a certification wasn't worth much unless one had the experience to go with it – and I had little more than a month of teaching experience under my belt. Just the other day did I finally manage to get hired somewhere. Unfortunately, all the little club could offer me was one class a week – for thirteen dollars... This amount wouldn't do much to improve my financial situation. My remaining option was to try finding work as a waitress. Naturally, since I had absolutely *no* experience in that field, I wasn't likely to be hired by one of the more respectable restaurants, at least not as fast as I needed to. And I doubted such establishments would even consider someone without a work permit anyway. No, in order to score something quickly I would have to seek out one of those shady bars located in the most crime-infested areas of D.C. – bars in which I knew from reading the newspaper every day murders weren't exactly uncommon... The thought of having to peddle drinks and/or food to the people patronizing these types of joints suddenly made me feel very cold and my mouth became dry. Well, working in a place like that was still better than having to return to Sweden, I soon concluded. And, as it was, I should at least give a couple of the better restaurants a chance before heading over to the dumps. Who knew, my bad luck so far in the D.C. job market might just have decided to make a big u-turn... So, when I returned home from school in the early evening, I grabbed the Washington Post, placed myself in one of the chairs in the living room, and began scanning the ads in the classifieds for a few good restaurants seeking waiters. And that was how I discovered women could make money selling their eggs.

Well, would it really be my child just because we were genetically related? I wasn't so sure about that. I mean, after all, it wasn't a matter of donating a *kid*, right? It wasn't like I would become a surrogate mother. If I did it, all that couple would ever get from me was an egg – a *cell*. It was kind of like giving someone one of my hairs. Then, later, that hair would become a child to whom I would merely be the *biological* mother, not the real mother, the one that counted. Because wasn't motherhood a bond that formed when you raised someone from babyhood? I thought so. Wasn't this the very reason adoptive parents claimed that their adopted children felt no less like "their" kids than any kids they might have given birth to? Definitely. So then it couldn't really be *my* kid... Heck, I didn't even have it in my stomach for nine months, so how could I ever consider it mine? In other words, all I would sell would be a tiny, tiny cell containing my genes. I couldn't see any problem in doing that.

I smiled to myself: Yes, this is what I should do. I should become an egg donor! Filled with renewed enthusiasm, I grabbed the cordless phone once more and got ready to punch in the number. In that moment, however, my eyes found the digital clock embedded into the VCR below the TV. I realized that it was past ten p.m. already. It probably wasn't so smart to call up someone at such a late hour. No, I better wait until tomorrow, I concluded and put the phone back down. I could only pray

I was feeling as confident then as I was now.

◥◤◢◣

The following day I sat outside my classroom next to a pay phone, having told the teacher I needed to visit the bathroom so that I could call the number in the ad undisturbed.

Of course, the high spirits from last night were but a distant memory now and instead I felt like I usually did in situations like these: nervous with a capital N followed by three exclamation marks. The skin on my arms sported goose bumps and the tight orange cotton top I wore had suddenly developed two large, very sweaty-looking stains right where my armpits were located. Having to make this important call in English, a language I wasn't all that great at yet and especially not under pressure, didn't exactly improve the state of my upset nerves. Telling myself to stop acting like such a wimp, I had a determined sip from the diet coke in one hand and began punching in the phone number with my other. As I waited for someone to answer, each ring reverberated inside my head with disturbing intensity. Dear God, please make me sound like a normal, not-just-off-the-boat person, I begged. Please let me not speak too fast or unclear. It took five rings before someone picked up.

"Hello," a woman's soft voice said.

Taking a deep breath, I spoke: "Hi, myy name is Julia Deerek and I'm caalinggg about de aad in de Waashington Post neewspaper about to become an eegg donor…"

"Excuse me?"

Oh, no… Apparently, I wasn't comprehensible at all. Godammit! As I said, I was well aware that my English wasn't topnotch yet, but I hadn't thought it was that bad either. Feeling the stains under my armpits grow larger, I cleared my throat and tried once more, taking even more care not to speak fast and to enunciate instead.

"Hi, *myyy naaame* is *Juuulia Deeerek* and *III*'m caaalinggg about de aad in de Waaashington Post Neeewspaper about to become an *eeeegg* donor…"

There was a slight pause on the other side of the line.

"Egg donor? You must have dialed the wrong number."

What? The wrong number? Confused, I brought the folded newspaper lying on the little brown table beneath the pay phone closer so that I could get a better view of the number listed in the ad. She was right; instead of the five in the end of the number, I had dialed a six.

"Oh, I'm sorry!" I said and rapidly hung up. So maybe my English wasn't quite *that* disastrous then...

Making sure I got each of the numbers right this time, I made a second attempt. A man answered on the third ring, and, swiftly, I rattled out the same line I had only seconds ago. Fortunately for me, the man immediately understood the purpose for my call.

After a few qualifying questions regarding my suitability as the biological mother of his future child – mostly verifying that I indeed had the physical aspects the ad required – he wondered if I could meet with him and his wife so that they could see and talk to me in person. Doing my best not to let my eagerness shine through, as I didn't deem too much eagerness appropriate, I said that weekdays after six o'clock worked best for me.

As soon as I hung up I had to constrain myself not to shout out loud. I did it! On Wednesday, two days later, I was going to meet with the people that would solve my problems.

▼▼▼

Unfortunately, it turned out that the Jamesons – the couple I met up with inside a busy fish restaurant – didn't want me as their donor. The main reason, they explained when we spoke on the phone a week after, was that Ms. Jameson and I hadn't resembled one another sufficiently in terms of facial features. This was true; the only thing we both had had in common was our eye color – a yellowy green. Other than that, we were about as similar as a cat to a dog. Her nose had been short and a little wide, turned upward like that of a child, whereas mine is quite thin and straight. The eyes had been large and protruding with heavy eyelids, the opposite of my deep-set, rather small eyes. Her mouth had been full and wide, dominating her heart-shaped face, unlike my broader one where the cheekbones and square jawbones are the most obvious features. And her hair had been a lot darker. Yet, despite having been perfectly aware of all of this, a tiny but fierce hope that they would pick me anyway had burned within me; after all, we did hit it off during our meeting and they had really seemed to like me.

Heavy with disappointment, I hung up the phone after having said good-bye to Ms. Jameson. That was *really* too bad… Oh well. Maybe if I kept reading the classifieds in the Washington Post, I would find another couple, I tried cheering myself. Surely, there must be plenty of others looking for donors. See, at this point, I couldn't get the notion that it was possible to get thousands of dollars for my eggs out of my head. Why become a waitress when you could become an egg donor? It just seemed like *such* an easy and great way to make money – and especially for a person like me, as marriage and having kids weren't things high up on my to-do list in life. All I wanted was to have a great career and a great boyfriend – in that order. Yes, so that's what I would do; I would find someone else to whom I would sell my eggs.

But after about six weeks of unsuccessful searching, I began to get seriously frustrated. The only people looking for a donor were one Asian couple and one couple that wanted kids of Jewish decent. Maybe these infertile couples weren't as common as I had imagined. Maybe the Jamesons had just been a *fluke*… Thank God that somewhere in the midst of this hunt I obtained a second, better-paying job teaching aerobics, which at least partially alleviated the stress I was going through.

Seated on a white plastic chair waiting for my class to start at this other gym, a health club located in Northeastern Washington D.C, I was like always lately carefully scanning the newspaper. It didn't take long, however, before I threw it back into the magazine bin, sighing out loud. A little too loud, I guess, because Anna, one of my most devoted students currently sitting next to me devouring a fitness magazine, gave me a worried look.

"Is everything OK, Julia?"

I looked at her, trying to determine whether it was a good idea or not to let her in on my secret obsession to become an egg donor. It was probably better if I kept my mouth shut, I concluded rapidly. Come to think of it, even though I had gotten to know her through my classes, I wasn't at all sure that she *wasn't* one of those super-religious pro-lifers who considered dabbling with a woman's procreative apparatus an unforgivable sin. I had read plenty about those people back in Sweden. But like on so many other occasions similar to this one, my brain refused to cooperate, forcing me to tell the truth – or at least part of it.

"Uuhh... Well, I was looking for an ad in de help-wanted section dat I couldn't find..."

"You're not going to leave us here and go somewhere else and teach, are you?" she blurted out, her rather narrow eyes suddenly changing, becoming round and big like two ping pong balls. "Because you're my favorite teacher, I don't like any of the other teachers, their classes are *sooo* boring. I'm so happy that you started teaching here. If you leave I don't know what to do..."

The words seemed to get stuck in her throat.

Touched by the rambling lobby for me to remain at the club, I put a hand on her shoulder and smiled.

"No, no, relax, I'm *not* going to quit at Paragon Fitness. I was looking for an ad about..." I paused. My head stood still. What could I come up with? I could tell by the expression on her face that I hadn't convinced her quite yet. Oh, screw it! I might as well just tell the truth. So I said, "I was looking for an ad about couples searching for egg donors."

She gave me an undefined glance.

"Egg donor? You want to become an egg donor? Why?"

"Because you can make lots of money doing it." The moment these words came out of my mouth, I regretted them. Now Anna would probably think that I'm a greedy asshole, I thought. The preferred answer – the one *good girls* state – would have been because I thought it was a nice thing to do for somebody. But, as it happens, I'm the worst liar in the universe. I got ready for a moral lecture.

"I think my cousin donated her eggs last year," she said instead, a faraway expression in her brown eyes that had now returned to their natural shape.

It took a couple of seconds for her unexpected answer to register in my brain.

"Really?" I finally got out. "How did she find her couple?" I was back on track.

"She didn't find the recipients for her eggs on her own. She went through an agency."

"An agency? Are dere agencies for egg donors? I didn't know dat!"

I didn't care if I might have sounded a little too excited, not now that I had finally found a lead as to how I would be able to sell my eggs.

"Yes, there is," she confirmed.

"Do you know where I can find out about dis agency?"

"I don't remember the name of it, but I can ask Linda. My cousin, that is. She'd know."

Anna kept her promise. A few days later, when it was time for another of my classes, she brought a little note that she held tightly in her hand. On it, the name and phone number of the agency were printed neatly.

It wasn't until I spoke to the egg donor coordinator of the Maryland Fertility Group that I found out that donating eggs wasn't exactly a simple process; on the contrary, it was *very* complicated. You didn't just go into a hospital one day, have your eggs somehow removed, and then, five minutes later, a fat check was issued in your name. For some strange reason, I had convinced myself of a scenario like this. (Or perhaps it wasn't so strange, considering that the only thing the Jamesons and I had discussed regarding the practical side of the procedure had been whether I had ever donated before and how long I was planning to stay in the area.)

At any rate, the coordinator – a tired-looking, extremely uptight woman dressed in a beige business suit – let me know that first of all I had to fill out an extensive questionnaire regarding my family history, health, and personality. This questionnaire was about forty pages thick. Then I would have to meet with some of the doctors who would evaluate whether I was suited to become a donor or not, as the Maryland Fertility Group was *very* particular when picking their donors. For example, they wanted to make sure they only picked women driven by a need to help infertile couples, not ones driven by monetary needs. As a matter of fact, only about 20 percent of all women applying to the clinic actually ended up one of their donors, the coordinator added haughtily. If I were lucky enough to pass this screening, the next step was to go through a rigorous physical examination to ensure I was perfectly healthy. I would also have to supply the agency with a few current photos of myself and, if possible, of myself as a child. I would have to see a lawyer that would take care of the legal aspects of the donation, and a psychologist had to approve me as well. Last, if they found a match for me, chances were high the prospective recipients would want to meet me before they would make their final decision.

I learned that there were quite a few drugs and hormones involved. For starters, we had something called Lupron. Both the recipient and I would have to take this drug intravenously so that our periods could be synchronized and my ovulation controlled (luckily for me, since my English wasn't particularly proficient at the time, I didn't fully grasp what it meant to take drugs intravenously). Later, when our menstrual cycles were in sync, it was time for other drugs, stimulating drugs that apparently would make my ovaries produce so many eggs I would be more than able to fill a miniature version of those styrofoam cartons containing a dozen eggs. When the eggs were deemed ripe for harvest, I would be put to sleep and the eggs would be surgically removed. "...all in all, this whole ordeal should be over within a few months, hopefully not more than three, but of course, since it would be your first time it's prudent to count on that we'll need at least four months from start to finish, maybe even five..."

My surprise must have been clearly expressed on my face because she stopped talking all of a sudden.

"Is everything all right, Ms. Derek?" she asked.

"Well, yah," I mumbled, "except dat I'm leaving D.C. in *less* dan four months. Would dat not give us enough time?"

It wouldn't.

This second failed attempt at donating my eggs hadn't been as disappointing to me as the one with the Jamesons despite that I had thought I *really* needed it to work out this time, or else I would have to hit those lethal bars. There had just been something about Mrs. Sanders – the uptight egg donor coordinator – that didn't sit well with me. Throughout the entire meeting she had been so cold and grumpy, to the point of being almost antagonistic, that I became convinced she must really not like me. The one time she had made an effort to smile, there had been a scowl between her eyebrows and, naturally, her stone-gray eyes had been unmoved during the effort. Furthermore, her claim that their agency only accepted women driven by a need to help people first, and not the ones coming primarily because of the sizeable monetary compensation, sounded a bit strange to me. If this indeed were the case, how would they enforce it? I guess they could start by not offering so much money.

More important, though, it wasn't a major economic catastrophe, as my financial hardship worked out by itself. Three days later I received some miraculous, very unexpected news: Due to the delinquent behavior of the main teacher in our journalism program, we, the students, were to be reimbursed 3,000 dollars each. This money was available in our accounts only two weeks from that moment.

2

SOUTHERN COMFORT

In June, four months later, I landed in Los Angeles, the city in which I had decided to continue my journalism studies. The decision to move here had not come easy; I had for a long while prior been torn between whether I should really head for California or if it wouldn't be better to go to New York instead. The two states were equally attractive to me but in widely different manners. For example, I found the fast pace and melting-pot status of New York City a huge turn-on. On the other hand, the consistently warm weather and the fact that Hollywood with all its glamour was located in California could not be easily overlooked. In the end, the West won, not only because I had become so exceedingly tired of having to endure the long, harsh winters served in places like Sweden, D.C., and New York, but also because my latent but ever-present urge to give the field of entertainment a shot had come to beckon for my attention more and more.

Sitting in our large living room in a brand-new dark red couch, my roommate Ilse and I were sipping on homemade Cosmopolitans, complimenting each other over and over regarding our superb bartending skills. Ilse was a nearly six-foot tall, cute, and slightly chunky girl from Norway. She had a sea of flowing blond curls and the obligatory Nordic transparent blue eyes to match. I had run into her the very first day I set foot on the campus of my new school, Santa Monica College, in which I would take care of my GED-requirements before continuing at maybe UCLA or USC. Considering that government-funded Scandinavians and BMW-driving Asians with orange and green hair invaded this campus, it wasn't a total coincidence that she happened to be from the same neck of the woods as I. Anyway, the two of us had clicked instantaneously upon which we began searching for a place to live together. Pretty soon we had found a nice one-bedroom apartment in Santa Monica that we could afford, and, as of today, we had occupied it for exactly three weeks and three days.

We had spent the entire day shopping for furniture and then brought it to our home, something we would have taken care of much sooner had our student money arrived on time. See, as I was no longer studying with a private organization that charged shameless prices for the privilege of attending their program – a program that, on top of it, had turned out to be full of problems and a crooked teacher – but a cheap community college, I could actually look forward to be able to use the not so modest financial aid I received from the Swedish government for things other than just tuition and rent. Of course, the non-resident status that came with being a foreigner required us to pay about ten times as much as residential students, so we weren't exactly swimming in money either... Still, I was happy because together with what we had received from the organizers, I had enough to make a decent living for the next couple of months. When that time was over, I was sure to have found a few jobs teaching aerobics, as in my arsenal now I had not only a lot more experience but also letters of glowing recommendation from my bosses back in D.C. And these days I was allowed to work on campus, though I didn't think I would end up doing that, as I was determined to give egg donation a third shot – *successful* this time. At any rate, up until today, Ilse and I had lived in an apartment that was completely empty except for our twin-sized mattresses and stands; therefore, now that we had a large couch to sit in, a couple of tables to put our stuff on, and a TV to watch, naturally, we had to celebrate with not one but *two* Cosmos each. Happy and a bit drunk, we admired through our opened balcony the postcard-like way in which the California sun was setting amongst a small congregation of palm trees.

"Er ikke det bare glimrende den solen?" Ilse said to me in Norwegian, a silly smile on her plump, raspberry-red lips.

"What?" I asked. "Stop speaking Norwegian to me, I don't understand it."

Ilse insisted on speaking Norwegian to me. Strangely enough, many Norwegians – and many Danes, too – seem to think that just because *they* have no problem understanding Swedish, we Swedes automatically will understand their poor excuses for a language, which are both substandard versions of Swedish (or, at any rate, that is what we Swedes think...). Well, most of us don't understand a word. I'm not sure why this is. Ilse claimed it is because the Norwegians are a brighter type of Scandinavians.

"I said 'Isn't that beautiful that sunset?'" Ilse repeated – albeit reluctantly – in English.

"Absolutely," I agreed, nodding so hard half my drink landed on my top instead of in my mouth. "Thank God I moved here instead of to New York."

"I love California, everything about it: the weather, the men, the beach, Hollywood, the nightlife, *everything*!" She paused briefly, looking out the opened balcony door once more. Then she continued. "I just wish I had some more money. My student money doesn't exactly go very far. I don't even want to think about how little money I have left after today what with all the stuff we bought. Of course, it was a necessary expense."

"I know what you mean; I feel exactly the same way. Well, maybe you can become an egg donor. Like I will." It wasn't until now, after having been in Santa Monica for over a month, that I had had a chance to even begin thinking about finding a clinic or an agency where I could donate. Before that, my hands had been full with... well, life. Relocating to a completely unknown part of this huge country on my own had been a little more laborious and complicated than what I had first expected.

Ilse looked at me with her big, blue, pretty eyes. That smile, which was usually painted on her face 24/7, died and a thoroughly confused expression replaced it.

"Egg donor?"

"Yes, you can donate your eggs and get thousands of dollars for it!" I could hardly believe this reality myself even as I said it. It didn't matter that the actual process was not by far as simple as I had first thought; it *still* seemed almost too good to be true.

"Really?" Confusion was exchanged for childlike expectation.

"Yes!!"

"Can I do that, too?"

"I don't see why not."

The following day, as I was calling a woman named Ruth McCall, Ilse was sitting next to me, eager to find out more about this potential goldmine. I had found Ruth's number by mistake while flipping through Backstage West, a trade paper for struggling actors, a day or so earlier in search of acting classes. (Like mentioned before, the need to find out if I had what it took to make it in the entertainment industry had become so big I had to acknowledge it – and acting was my vehicle of choice.) Actually, I had found quite a few people advertising for girls willing to give up their eggs for money in this paper; apparently, waiting tables had gotten some serious competition as the actress' preferred means of income. Ruth's ad had looked most compelling though, and, to tell the truth, the fact that she offered, as she put it "a generous compensation", didn't make it less compelling.

When a high-pitched voice answered the phone, I asked to speak to Ruth McCall. I didn't have to wait long before a woman with a marked Southern lilt announced that her name was indeed that. Her warm voice embodied everything that Southern hospitality implied. I cleared my throat slightly before speaking, feeling less nervous than usual thanks to Ilse sitting next to me for moral support. Also, by now my English was better and it was no longer the first time I was calling somebody regarding this matter.

"Hi, my name is Julia Derek and I'm calling about the egg donor ad."

"Are yew loo'king to become a donor?"

"Yes, I am."

"Oh, that sounds just gr'eaaat! Now pu'leeez allow me to ask yew a few questions then."

"Sure."

"How old are ya, honey?"

"I became twenty-five a couple of months ago."

"Where is that bee'yoo'tiful ak'syent from?"

"Sweden."

I hadn't yet figured out for sure if one was required to have a work permit in order to donate eggs, but since the issue had never come up I seriously doubted it. *If* it were a prerequisite, now would be the time to ask for it. Chances were that anybody with a thick accent like mine probably wasn't born with one.

"Oh, I see," was all she said.

I stifled a loud sigh of relief. But I was not allowed to relax quite yet. The next question would definitely take me aback.

"Have you ever had any abortions?"

What did *that* matter? As it was, I *had* had an abortion while studying in Spain three years earlier. I wasn't sure if this was such a smart thing to admit though, at this early, highly vulnerable stage of our relationship. Back in D.C., when I had gone to see the woman at the Maryland Fertility Group, we hadn't ever gotten into personal matters. The whole meeting had been more of a general information one. During a moment of major paranoia, I became convinced that Ruth was trying to trick me in some way, maybe to determine whether I was a slut or not – a slut who, on top of it, wasn't careful enough to use protection when she slept around. They probably didn't want any slutty girls to be their donors. Or maybe it meant that women who had had an abortion for some reason weren't physically capable of becoming egg donors. Of course, that didn't make any sense because most of those women had no problem whatsoever getting pregnant later on in life. What should I say? All these thoughts went through my head in a matter of seconds. Well, I concluded at last, I might as well just tell the truth. If it turns out she thinks I'm a slut, so be it. Rather a slut than a liar anyway, I almost managed to convince myself. Here we go...

"Yes, I have had an abortion, three years ago." No longer trying to pretend that I didn't care, I squeezed my eyes shut and prayed that my honesty wouldn't disqualify me.

"Oh, that's gr'eaaat!"

Great? What was so great about it, I wondered confused.

"That means that your fertility has been proven. It's so much easier to match donors who've had their fertility proven."

Oh, I see. Thank God that I'm an almost pathologically honest person – too honest for my own good many times.

"Oh, OK."

"When can you come in to the office here so we can meet up?"

"Uhhh..." I tried to think of how soon I would be able to come in. Tomorrow, around two p.m. in between classes would be the best, I determined. "I can make it tomorrow after two p.m."

"How about two-thirty tomorrow? Does that sound awl'right?"

"Two-thirty sounds perfect!"

She gave me the address to the clinic. As we were about to hang up, Ilse pinched the skin on my bare arm.

"Oh, one more thing, Ma'am," I hurried saying before Ruth would hang up.

"Call me Ruth, please, honey, Julia. Ma'am makes me feel like an ol' lady!"

"Oh, OK....uuhm...*Ruth*. I have a friend here next to me who wants to become a donor, too. Can she talk to you?"

"Why shooor, put her on!"

3

NECESSARY (SHARP) EVIL

I arrived at the West Los Angeles Medical Center, which contained Ruth's office, a few minutes later than what we had agreed upon. I had walked all the way from my school to the Center and even though it wasn't located particularly far away, it had still taken quite a bit longer than what I had calculated. (It was during this time I discovered that I was terrible at judging distances on a map.) See, during that first summer in Santa Monica I was struggling to take my driver's license test. This was something I should have completed years ago in Sweden; however, since I had always lived in places where you got around just fine without a car, I had kept postponing it. I learned rapidly that in Santa Monica, which is part of the greater Los Angeles metropolitan area, you *had* to have a car – unless you preferred spending seven hours a day waiting for infrequent buses that were jam-packed, rarely on time, and delivered you to your preferred destination ten times slower than a guy on a bike delivered pizza to your house. This sad reality wasn't because the L.A. Metropolitan Transportation Authority was equipped with slower-moving buses than other American cities, but because what people consider Los Angeles is extremely spread out. It is not a traditional city with a heart but a cluster of many small ones (like Santa Monica) in between which people drive miles and miles on the many freeways that connect these cities; hence, the famous smog. And, due to the ever-impending earthquake risk, there wasn't much of a subway system. Therefore, the most efficient way to get from point A to point B was by car. Of course, just being *aware* of that didn't help me much when I finally tired of waiting for a bus that never showed up.

Sweaty – and irritated from being covered in exhaust from top to toe

– I burst through the white door leading in to the clinic's waiting room, hoping that I hadn't hurt my chances to become a donor. I stumbled up to the receptionist's window and announced my presence and the purpose for it. She told me to have a seat and that Ruth would soon be there.

Doing as I was told, I flopped down on a light green canvas sofa.

Sitting there, relaxing and catching my breath, I took sneak peaks at some of the other people occupying the soothing space. Two seats away from me a couple sat, holding hands and whispering amongst each other. Both of them were somewhere in their early forties, dressed in jeans and sweaters and big smiles. Opposite me, a girl about my age sat, flipping through a shiny issue of *People Magazine*. A nurse appeared in a doorway that seemed to be leading further into the clinic. She looked directly at the girl and called out, "Linda, Dr. Nixon is ready to see you." The girl stood up and disappeared with the nurse. Only when they were both well out of sight, it struck me that perhaps this girl was an egg donor, too. Then, in one of the corners of the room, I saw a brown-haired woman about thirty-five years old sitting hunched up. She stared before her with empty eyes. The skin on her face was white and transparent like skim milk and her shoulder-length hair looked as if it had lost all life, like the leaves of a plant in desperate need for water. Her lipstick-free lips were firmly pressed together. I remembered wondering what could have happened to her that made her look so miserable. But I didn't get to ponder it for long because a few moments later a short blond woman appeared in the doorway, her eyes finding mine as if we already knew each other. A big grin cracked up her rather long face and, as she said my name, it was more of a confirming statement than a question to find out whether or not I was I. Though a bit tentative, I returned her smile.

"Yes, that's me," I said.

Having taken no more than two large steps, she was standing before me – an act that appeared impossible for a person of her stature. (She only measured at the most five feet two inches.) Both her hands stretched out in a gesture to greet me.

"Julia, it's a plaaa'zhur to meet yew. I'm Ruth."

I extended my hand, which she covered with both hers.

"It's nice to meet you, too," I said, feeling slightly awkward. Her straightforward manner and profuse warmth threw me off balance despite having experienced a sample of it during our phone conversation two days earlier. She certainly appeared to be the polar opposite of that other, ice queen-like coordinator on the East Coast.

"Follow me," Ruth said, inviting me to walk with her to her office.

While engaging in small talk, we walked along a narrow corridor that seemed as if it never would end, taking sudden, almost illogical turns, kind of like a labyrinth. We passed a series of offices with their doors ajar. I did my best not to give in to my natural inclination, which was to peek inside of them.

"Here we are," Ruth said as we reached a tiny but very office-looking room. We stepped inside and she told me to take a seat. As she pulled out a drawer and dipped her hands inside it, I sat down next to her desk. She must have found what she was looking for because a content "Aha!" flew out from between her fuchsia-colored lips seconds later. She pulled out a thick stack of papers and proceeded to take a seat behind her desk.

"Julia, Julia," she began, that big grin back, even larger this time around. "So you want to become an egg donor?"

I nodded eagerly, but not too eagerly I hoped.

"Is this the first time you're donating?"

"Yes."

"Do you know anything about the process?"

I explained to her that I had been familiarized with it back in D.C., at another clinic.

"So you are aware of the fact that there's quite a lot of work on the donor's part then?"

I nodded somberly

"A lot of visits to the clinic?"

Again, I nodded. I hoped I would have my driver's license and a car by the time I would start.

"You know that you'll have to inject yourself with different types of fertility drugs? Hormones?"

I stopped mid-nod, as Ruth suddenly produced an enormously painful-looking needle from a little white box on her desk. The actual part that you were supposed to stick into your flesh measured about two entire inches. For the first time I seriously reconsidered my adamant decision to become an egg donor.

I must have looked pretty shocked because Ruth placed a hand on my shoulder and laughed apologetically (albeit with a hint of mischief).

"I'm so sorry, Julia, I didn't mean to scare you. I shouldn't have shown you this one first. The initial shots you will be taking are *a whole lot* tinier." She dug into her white box again and pulled out a series of – true to her statement – a whole lot tinier needles, wrapped in plastic and attached one to the other. "Are you scared of needles?" she asked.

"Yeah, I can't say I like them at all," I said, not even slightly ashamed to admit what a sissy I was.

"Don't you worry, sweetie, you won't have to inject all of this large needle. Only about a half of it," she added, as if that was supposed to be some kind of consolation, showing me the nail-resembling needle again. "Or you can have a friend do it. A lot of my donors have their roommates do it. In the worst case you can always come to the clinic and a nurse will do it for you."

"I'm sure I can handle them," I mumbled.

"I don't doubt that for a second!" Ruth agreed. "You seem like a girl that can handle almost anything." She let out a merry laugh, spurring me to laugh as well.

It struck me how much I really liked Ruth and her feisty personality. She was anything but uptight. She made me relax completely, as if I was talking to an old friend instead of to the gatekeeper to my ovarian riches. And if this was some kind of audition to determine whether I was a good candidate to become a donor for her clinic, I felt as if I had already passed it with glory a long time ago. As she kept speaking, reiterating some of the things I already knew from having spoken to that other woman back East, I contemplated her surreptitiously. She was wearing a black and white jersey dress. Though somewhere around forty she was still pretty, you could tell that as a young woman, she must have been *very* pretty. She was the type of person that smiled with every part of her face when she smiled and, like Ilse, she smiled a lot. Her large eyes were dark blue and enclosed by a thick layer of black mascara-coated eyelashes. They were set fairly deeply in a face that was almost, but only almost, too narrow to be really attractive. She had a small nose, perfect teeth like Farrah Fawcett, and rather thin lips dressed in bright fuchsia.

"…in terms of risks, there aren't really any to speak of. According to one study done in the eighties there is a very, very slight chance that ovarian cancer is triggered by stimulating a person's ovaries through the intake of these hormones, but plenty of other studies entirely refute this finding. In other words, there's really nothing to worry about."

"Oh, OK," I said. The other egg coordinator had given me the same information.

"There might be some discomfort after the eggs are retrieved. You might experience some pain and swelling, very similar to premenstrual symptoms. But that should pass after a few days – at the most a week. Chances are you won't have any side effects at all."

I nodded, even though I could not relate to PMS. Hard as it is to believe, I had never ever experienced anything even remotely unpleasant with my period. No cramps, no bloating, no headaches, no depression, no being overly emotional, no nothing. As a matter of fact, I was always surprised when I discovered that this month's period had arrived. And then what little blood came hardly lasted three days. Women always told me how lucky I was. My stock answer to this was, "No, I'm not lucky; I'm just part *male*".

"Do you have any questions of your own?" Ruth asked.

She had not yet told me how much money I was supposed to receive. I figured that now was a good time to bring that up without the risk of sounding too greedy. Remembering what she had written in the ad, I expected her to say something in the 4,000-dollar range.

"2,500 dollars."

What? Was that all? In D.C. the woman had offered 3,500 dollars – just like the Jamesons. And in one of the other ads in the Backstage West somebody had offered as much as 5,000.

"Hmmm," was all I could say to this.

Ruth continued, unfazed by my reaction: "And that's tax exempt of course since it's a donation, so you don't need to have a work permit."

Well, thank God for that. At least I didn't have to worry about the eligibility of my status as a foreigner.

"Anything else?"

Though knowing it might not come off overly altruistic if I demanded to know how come there was such a disparity in compensation between the different agencies, my urge to find out the answer was too big.

"How come Pacific Fertility Agency pays less than some other clinics? I'm sorry if it sounds as if money is very important to me, but I did see that a couple of other places pay almost the double…" Even though I really liked and felt I could trust Ruth, I didn't think the time was ripe enough for me to admit that money was the motivation for me to donate, not altruism (which I figured was the one reason she would prefer to hear if she would ask).

"Actually, we pay what most reputable clinics in California pay, believe it or not, some pay even less. I know which ads you're talking about, and I know the doctors they employ. They aren't nearly as skilled as the doctors here, nor do they have a lot of experience. Dr. Nixon, the person in charge of this clinic, is one of the doctors that created and pioneered the entire donation procedure. So you can be assured you're thoroughly safe in our hands."

Ruth did have an excellent point; I would rather make a little less money in exchange for not having to worry about whether or not I would still be alive after the donation was over. I nodded, understanding.

"You will also have to see a psychologist."

That was right, the psychologist. I had wondered what that was for. "Why is that?"

"Oh, it's just standard procedure. All the girls have to go through a psychological screening to make sure they're emotionally stable before they are allowed to donate. It's really nothing; the only thing you have to do is talk to our psychologist for a few minutes and then it's over. But I'm sure you won't have any kind of trouble."

I didn't quite know how to react to Ruth's answer. It made sense – but at the same time it didn't make any sense at all. I didn't know why and I didn't know if my feelings were valid, but I did feel kind of insulted by it.

"I see," was all I said.

We spoke some more. She let me know that the procedure wouldn't in any way impede or reduce my chances to have my own kids in the future. Then she handed me a thick questionnaire, which she told me to fill out as soon as possible. The sooner it is done, the faster we can get you started, she emphasized. There was information regarding the procedure I needed to read over that she handed me. I had to sign informed consents. Then she let me know that she thought it would be very easy to find a match for me, so we might as well set up an appointment for me to have my physical right away. And of course, I would have to provide her with some flattering photos of myself.

An hour had passed when we stood up to say good-bye.

"Well, it shooore was nice to meet yew, Julia," Ruth said, shaking my hand and, like before, smiling with her entire face.

I couldn't have agreed more. I shook her hand firmly and, two seconds later, I positively floated out of her office, euphoric from the thought that I would soon become 2,500 dollars richer.

〜〜〜

"Hvordan var det? Hva skjedde?" Ilse almost shouted at me in her mother tongue, attacking me as soon as I stepped inside our apartment an hour later. "Skal du gjøre det?"

"What?" I said in English, dropping my bag with all my schoolbooks on the floor. Finally getting rid of those extra thirty pounds I had been dragging around all day long made me feel as if I was suddenly airborne.

"Speak English, I don't understand Norwegian!"

"Maybe if you stopped telling yourself that, you would understand!" Ilse countered in English. "It's not that different from Swedish."

"It is too!" I threw myself down on our large couch and stretched out every limb and closed my eyes. "Uuuuhh, you don't know how much I've missed this sofa, Ilse…"

I could hear Ilse take a seat on a chair next to the sofa. She grabbed my hand and pulled it decisively.

"Don't fall asleep before you tell me what happened! What did you have to do? When are you gonna donate?"

Reluctantly, I opened one of my eyes and peered at the excited Norwegian woman by my side.

"It doesn't work like that, Ilse," I explained. "First you have to fill out tons of paper work about yourself, and you have go through different tests, and then, *if* you pass the tests, they have to match you with somebody before you can start. It's not that simple."

Ilse shrugged her shoulders, as if what I had just told her wasn't really an issue.

"What about the money? How much money are they gonna pay?"

"2,500 dollars."

"Really? That's great! That will take care of all my tuition fees this semester."

At this point in the conversation both of my eyes were opened and I was half sitting up, supporting my upper body with one of my elbows. I contemplated Ilse. The expression on her face changed abruptly, as if something suddenly had hit her.

"What?" I asked.

"I wonder if you can do it more than one time."

"I'm pretty sure you can do it a few times."

Yet again Ilse's facial expression metamorphosed, now becoming very serious.

"If I can make 8,000 dollars donating my eggs, I won't have to take out a student loan at all to cover my last year at Santa Monica. 8,000 together with the scholarship will be more than enough to get by. That would be so great."

"That would be pretty cool," I agreed. "When is your appointment with Ruth again?"

"On Monday at nine a.m."

"You're going to like her a lot. She's really cool."

We spent the rest of the evening dreaming, coming up with different ways on how to spend all the money we would make selling our eggs. And, for once, the future would prove to be as good as our dreams.

4

CROSS-EXAMINATION

The following day, a Saturday, I was lying in my twin-sized bed eating breakfast and filling out the last pages of the questionnaire. It was ten a.m. and I had woken up a few minutes earlier, still feeling tired. In my eagerness to comply with Ruth's suggestion that the sooner I would return the completed questionnaire the sooner I could start, I had stayed up until four a.m. the night before to finish all the papers. To claim that I was now *very* grumpy was not an exaggeration; I had only received slightly more than half of the eight hours of sleep I needed to function well the next day. Despite going to bed as soon as I discovered what time it was, I had been too wound up to be able to fall asleep. I couldn't get the questionnaire out of my head. There had just been so *many* questions in it, questions asking for the weirdest things. And some had struck me as rather irrelevant. For example, I just couldn't figure out what my religion had to do with anything. It wasn't like being Catholic or Protestant or atheist or whatever one were was hereditary. Nor was my sexual orientation (which is straight), unless it had recently been proven for sure that homosexuality indeed was congenital. They also wanted to know what my favorite animal was and my favorite color. Those questions just *had* to be some sort of trick questions, because what difference did it really make whether I preferred blue or black or red, elephant or bird? Or did it actually say something about you? Maybe it did… I think I managed to fall asleep sometime while trying to make that one out.

The one window in my and Ilse's sparsely furnished room revealed that it was a gorgeous day outside. The Santa Monica sun spilled all over our room, efficiently highlighting the areas that needed to be dusted. It seemed to me that no matter how much you cleaned this darn apartment, it never got clean enough – or at least not entirely free of dust. Not that a microscopically thin residual layer of dust bothered me very much, to be totally honest. The only person bothered by it was Ilse, the clean freak. Every morning, instead of enjoying the beautiful sunshine that woke us up, she went ballistic at the sight of the left-over particles of dust and ran into the bathroom where she fetched a damp cloth and began scrubbing the surfaces of our chest of drawers and her drawing table and chair. After about a week of this behavior I knew that she and I, even though I liked her a lot and we did have a lot of fun together, weren't meant to be roommates.

At any rate, here I lay, struggling with the seemingly never-ending pages, where I was not merely supposed to give a thorough description of myself covering every area one could imagine, but of my family, too; their height, their weight, hair and eye color, a thorough and detailed documentation of their health were but some of the data requested. And not just for the immediate relatives like my mom and dad and my big brother. No, as I discovered the night before when I had spent forty minutes conscientiously filling out the three pages each about my parents and listlessly flipped through the next twenty pages, apparently they needed to know the minutiae of my family tree down to when the human race was part gorilla. Grandparents, aunts, uncles, nephews, nieces, first cousins, second cousins, you name it. (OK, maybe not *second* cousins, but still. Who keeps track of your uncle's weight?) This requirement was made even more demanding since the last time I actually met any of my father's family members was something like twenty-two years ago – and I can't say I remember all that much from my life as a three-year-old. Not too many years thereafter both my father's grandparents passed away from old age. To make matters worse, my mother and father divorced on extremely bad terms when I was five, resulting in me not spending a whole lot of time with my dad, which in turn was the reason I didn't get to spend any time at all with his family. Therefore, I can't claim that I know much about them. But, as luck will have it, my dear mother happens to be the most family-oriented person on earth. She got to know my father's family quite well. My problems were easily solved by giving her a ring, which I did very late the previous night, as the time difference between Sweden and California is nine hours. I also had to tell her to dig up some baby photos that she could send me.

My mother hadn't been nearly as convinced as I that selling your eggs for money was the greatest thing in the world.

"...but Julia, are you sure this is safe?" she said in what to her was meant to be a concerned tone. To me it sounded more like a *whiny* tone.

"Yes, mom," I replied, wondering how many more times I had to go over the procedure with her before she would understand it was all but perfectly safe.

"Yes, but what if you can't have any children later when you find a husband? Maybe I won't ever have any grandkids!"

"That's not an issue at all, mom. Nobody who's been an egg donor has ever had any problems having kids later. I've read about this on the Internet. Besides, you know I don't really want to have any kids of my own, so it doesn't really matter."

"Yes, but Julia, you say that now, when you're older you might change your mind. Maybe you want to have a big family when you're thirty-five. What if you become the first egg donor that can't have children?"

"I *highly* doubt that."

"Yes, but Julia, why don't you get a job instead?"

"Mom, do you remember that I'm Swedish? Swedish citizens are not allowed to *work* in America. Of course, I'll do that anyway. I'll find a place where I can teach aerobics, just like I did in D.C. But that won't be enough."

"Yes, but Julia, why do you need so much money anyway? Isn't the student loan enough?"

"No, unfortunately it won't be enough. Besides, is there a thing as too much money...?" I laughed mischievously.

"Julia!" my mother exclaimed, ever the righteous mother, even though I knew that deep inside, having grown up in poverty, she completely and thoroughly agreed with me. "Don't talk like that! If it's going to give you problems later on, you shouldn't do it. What do you need all that money for anyway?"

"Oh, I can think of about a thousand things I can spend that money on. Maybe you can give me some money if you think it's so bad." This was a blow below the belt, I knew, as my mother didn't have a lot of money to spare.

"No, Julia. I grew up with much less money than you, and I survived just fine. And we had to work so much we hardly had time to go to school. Unlike you and your brother. You just have to learn to economize better. You're not a kid anymore." My mother loved bringing up her tough childhood whenever there was an opportunity.

"Yeah, yeah." I was getting tired of discussing the pros and cons of egg donation, as I had made up my mind as it was. "So tell me about dad's parents now..."

But my mother wasn't quite ready yet. There were still a few things she had to add.

"Why don't you find yourself a rich man and get married, Julia? That way you don't have to work. Now that you're in Hollywood and everything, it shouldn't be that hard to find a rich guy."

"Mom, you know I'm not the type to marry for money."

"Well, change then. I wish I would have done that, so I didn't have to work in a factory."

"Uh huh. What if I marry a rich guy and then I can't stand him? What if I don't like him?"

"You can learn to like him, Julia."

My mother is definitely one of a kind.

I went over the family information she had helped me include once more to make sure that it looked OK. Since it had been written down rather rapidly and since it had been three a.m. at the time – not my most focused period of the day – chances were I had made a few mistakes. It turned out, though, that I had managed to get it all down in a presentable fashion.

It amazed me how healthy my relatives appeared to be. I had never really thought about this before. In Sweden we eat lots of plain yogurt in paper boxes featuring photos of 120-year-old Russian guys with cone-like woolen helmets on their heads. Evidently we are supposed to buy into the notion that these durable shepherds have reached their respectable age due to copious intakes of the sour substance (from what I understand yogurt is about as popular in Russia as vodka). Maybe the producers of these yogurt cartons should consider putting photos of my family there instead, under the headline "Healthiest Family of Russia" since my mother's side of the family all stem from Ukraine, which is next door to Russia. We might not be as old yet, but most of us definitely do not look like raisins or sport funny hats. Surely, that would send the yogurt sales through the roof... Anyway, back to what we were talking about; namely, my family's health status, which apparently was excellent. None of us had died from cancer or suffered from any genetic mental illnesses. Nobody had been born disabled, nobody had Diabetes or Alzheimer's or Parkinson's or some other terrible, often hereditary disease. Nobody was obese; in fact, the majority was rather tall and lanky. Nobody had died young from unknown causes or experienced any heart attacks. It seemed as if the biggest health disaster ever hitting us was my big brother's acne attack as a teenager or my own nearsightedness.

When I was done going over the family section, I returned to the part covering me and my personality, grades, interests, special skills, talents, and so on. By now, almost all of it was filled out. Only a few questions were missing still.

I think I stared at the neatly typed headline "Describe your personality truthfully and in detail. Include both good and bad qualities." for at least a couple of minutes straight. Normally, when people ask me, I have no problem whatsoever telling them what I'm like, but now I couldn't think of a single adjective that would describe me. (The fact that my lack of sleep had given me a major headache didn't make this any easier.) I couldn't even think of any bad adjectives. I felt that it was crucial that anything I put down sounded...appropriate. Or perhaps benign was a better word. Even my more negative qualities needed to sound benign.

For example, even though at times, like today when I hadn't slept well, I could be a major bitch, I didn't think that it was a good idea to put down "bitchy". I also felt that I should be as thorough and specific as possible, because I assumed that the recipient of my egg would want me to be close to her not merely physically but also in terms of temperament.

It took two more minutes of gnawing on the tip of my black ballpoint pen before I finally came up with an adjective that I deemed acceptable: "Strong". I'm not sure exactly what I meant by that, only that I have kind of a strong personality. Of course, since it wasn't entirely clear to me it wouldn't be particularly clear to the persons reading my profile. I better elaborate a little. Hmmm… "Strong – both physically and mentally". Yes, that sounded good and it was true too. OK, what else…what do people tell me about me usually…. Funny! People tell me that I'm fun to hang out with. But does that necessarily mean that you are a *funny* person…? Well, I think I'm pretty funny, so I will put down funny. Hmmm…what else…. I'm not an idiot. I should put down that I'm not completely brain dead. Smart was definitely a great genetic selling point and since my grades were all good, from grade school to college, it meant I even had the credentials to back up this claim. But then the ever-present Swede in me woke up, the one that revolted against any brazen, overly positive assertions of me as a person: If I put down that I'm strong, funny, and smart, don't I also come off as if I'm all full of myself? Could I really make such statements about myself? I decided I could and moved on (come to think of it, anyway, I guess I'm a little full of myself). Hmm…passionate! I'm very much a passionate person. Suddenly it seemed as if I were on a roll. Maybe this wasn't as hard as I had thought… Outgoing! Independent. I thought some more. And some more. But nothing else came to mind.

"Julia!" Ilse screamed from the kitchen. "Can I have the rest of your OJ?"

"Go right ahead!" I screamed back, at the same time as it hit me that I could ask Ilse about my personality. It should be a breeze for her to give me the lowdown on that.

"Ilse?"

"Yeah..." Her answer came out somewhat muddled.

"What are you doing?"

"...drinking your OJ and cleaning the apartment! What did you think I was doing?"

"Can you come here a sec? I need to ask you something..."

I heard a glass being put down rather firmly on that metallic surface next to the sink in the kitchen. Rapid footsteps approached our bedroom. And then Ilse was standing in the doorway, her mane of curly blond hair gathered somewhat messily on top of her head. The bright sunlight that flooded into the room and surrounded her made her appear angelic – if only for a few moments. It didn't matter that she was wearing a T-shirt that should have been thrown out many years ago, a pair of men's stained khaki shorts, and that both her hands were covered by those yellow plastic cleaning gloves.

"What do you want?"

Looking at Ilse standing there saint-like and all, ready to give the apartment one of her almost daily cleaning blitzes, made me feel even more lazy than normal. Rapidly, I jotted down the word "Lazy" on the questionnaire.

"What type of person am I, Ilse?"

She put her hands to the side and gave me an indefinable look – not quite annoyed but certainly not amused. She didn't much like being disturbed when she was in her cleaning-mode.

"What do you mean 'what type of person am I?' You're an OK person. A little lazy and messy, but otherwise you're OK."

"I can't put that down: 'I'm kind of lazy and messy, but otherwise I'm OK'. That doesn't sound very good."

Ilse glanced at the thick stack of papers next to me in the bed.

"Are you *still* working on that? I thought you finished it last night. How long is it? I hate filling out forms."

"Well, let me tell you, it's *long*. And they want so many details about *every*thing!" I let out a frustrated sigh. "Right now I'm on the part that deals with my personality. Thank God I'm done with all the relatives. I'm supposed to describe what type of person I am and I'm stuck. Can't think of a single thing."

Ilse crossed her arms and leaned into the right side of the doorway, looking pensive. You could almost see how her brain was working, trying to come up with some words to describe me.

"Ambitious!" I almost shouted, as this very illustrative quality of mine suddenly popped into my head. "Lively!" There came another one. Quickly, before I would forget them again, I jotted them down. And I qualified the word "Lazy" by writing "a bit" before it.

Ilse was still just standing there, as pensive as ever. I looked at her. "So?" I asked.

Ilse shook her head.

"I can't think of anything," she said.

I lifted my eyebrows.

"I didn't think it was *that* hard to come up with a few things about my personality! Maybe I don't even *have* a personality," I added grumpily.

"Sorry, I'm just not that good at this." Ilse scrunched up her face, making one last effort it seemed to convince me that I wasn't just a beating heart surrounded by some meat and bones and a layer of skin. Her eyes lit up.

"You're funny!"

I grimaced.

"Thanks, but that one I have down already."

Ilse shrugged and turned around, leaving me to my own devices.

Having pondered myself and my personality (which, for the first time in my life, I disputed even existed) some more, I finally decided that I could work on the personality part later, when I felt more inspired and I was less tired and grumpy. I turned the page and discovered to my relief that I had reached the next to the last one. But my relief wouldn't last long. On the top of this page the question I had dreaded would appear at some point appeared. I had dreaded it because I had quickly come to understand, starting with the Maryland Fertility Group, which answer was expected from an egg donor and I knew I would have a major problem playing along with it. (I doubted that PFA was any different in their requirements, though, admittedly, I didn't know this for a fact. Either way, *now* wasn't the time to take any chances.) On this page they wanted me to explain *why* I wanted to donate my eggs. They had devoted half a page for the answer.

Well, I sighed. I might as well go ahead and answer right away. The supposedly correct answer. I was supposed to explain here how wonderful I thought it was to help a childless couple have the child they had dreamed about for so long or something like that. Of course – don't get me wrong – I *did* think it was a wonderful thing that my eggs could create so much joy for someone else, that by doing this I might fulfill someone's biggest dream. That part was all good. But it wasn't my reason for choosing to donate. It had always been for the money. Would I even have *considered* it if it hadn't been for the money? Only if it would have been for a very dear friend or the sister I wasn't fortunate enough to have. Would I even have seen the ad in the Washington Post that one day more than seven months ago if they hadn't printed 3,500 dollars in big, black block letters? Probably not. And probably nobody else would either. The Jamesons had known this. They had known that, at the heart of it all, this was a business transaction.

But I was not going to put down that the prospect of making a few grand was my main motivation, as, clearly, nobody wanted to hear the bitter truth, the uncomfortable reality of it all. So I had to pretend that I was more of a saint than I really was. Instead of my truthful incentive, I put down a short and sweet: "I want to become a donor because it feels great to help someone who can't have a child to have a child." That was enough, I thought while contemplating it. I had made sure that I had written large letters so as to fill up more space.

That wasn't so bad, Julia, was it? I tried telling myself as I did my best to shake off the intense discomfort I begun to experience. But the feeling refused to disappear. For a long time I just stared at what I had written on that paper before me. And then, slowly, it became clear to me why I felt this way. It became abundantly clear, so clear it was as if the words screamed at me out loud from their white background: *You phony! You hypocrite!* I couldn't handle phonies and hypocrites. All my life I had run my own personal crusade against everything I thought flaunted one or both of these two qualities.

The more I thought about how I felt forced to act phony and hypocritical, the more irritated I got. My grouchiness reached an all morning high. Why did I even have to answer this question? I was convinced that I wasn't the only woman that did it for the money. Actually, I knew that I wasn't. The woman vacuuming our living room carpet so thoroughly you would think her life depended on that not even *one* dust particle remained was another. Surely, there were plenty of others. As a matter of fact, I was willing to put money on it that just about *every* woman did it for the money.

Why was this extremely personal question even here? I could definitely not see how it was *any* of their business the reasons that somebody wanted to donate their eggs. Nobody would be so stupid to write, "Because I need some extra cash." anyway. Wasn't it sufficient that a woman was nice enough to sell them her eggs? Now they wanted her dignity as a human being, too, forcing her to act like some kind of selfless puppet. I was fuming by now. Did it really matter *why* someone chose to donate their eggs as long as they did it voluntarily? I seriously doubted that the quality of the eggs would be affected by either the reason or the answer. And if they would be, in that case, what was worse when one thought about it: an egg with self-respect or an egg without a spine – that, on top of it, most likely was also acting phony? I thought there was no question about that one.

I had to laugh at myself eventually, at my sudden incensed state of mind. There was really no reason for me to be this upset. Who was I kidding? Now that I thought about it, hadn't I suspected more or less from the beginning that playing the game was one of the requirements if you wanted to become an egg donor? I had. That was just the way it was and either you followed the rules or you didn't donate. It was as simple as that. And, come to think of it, things weren't all that bad. Ruth, for example, didn't seem like a phony at all. That was probably why I had taken a liking to her so fast.

At the sight of the next question – which was the last one – my anger was soon forgotten. It said, "Do you wish to be an anonymous donor?" That was a tough one. I had never thought about this. Did I want to be anonymous? I tried to project into the future, say twenty or thirty years ahead. I highly doubted this would ever happen, but *if* a person would stand on my doorstep and tell me that I was his or her biological mother, how would I feel about it? Would it upset me? I wasn't sure. (But I did know that it wouldn't kill me.) It was too weird to even imagine. I guess I should just put that I preferred being anonymous. But as I was about to write this down, it struck me, What if I had been the child of an egg donor? I'm sure that *I* would have wanted to know at some point who my biological mother was. It must be pretty tough having to go through life forever curious about it. Come to think of it, didn't the donor have a kind of moral responsibility *not* to be anonymous? It seemed to me that they did. Then, the more I thought about it, the more I became convinced that I probably wouldn't be all that upset if the child that had resulted from my egg would want to see me. What was so upsetting about it really? Wasn't it actually kind of cool to meet this person? I think I would think so. I put down that I had no problem meeting my offspring if they would like to in the future. The second I put down the pen Ilse screamed at me to come help her sweep the balcony.

5

ON MY WAY...

"**H**i, Julia, how are ya doin', honey?" Ruth's signature drawl spoke on the other side of the phone line. "I have some good news. We've got a match!"

"Really? I was beginning to think nobody wanted my eggs," I answered. Ruth knew exactly what I was talking about.

Over two months had passed since the day when I returned my carefully filled out questionnaire for potential recipients to read. Like I had never doubted from the beginning, Ruth and the Pacific Fertility Agency definitely wanted to work with me. I had gone through the physical exam without a hitch; apparently, I was as healthy as the rest of my clan. I had signed all the necessary papers, renouncing any claims to the child produced from our efforts. For some reason, though, my compulsory visit to the psychologist kept being postponed. Not that I minded, of course. To be completely honest, I hoped that Ruth would forget all about me going there ever, for I really didn't feel like going. There was just something weird about having to see a psychologist because I wanted to donate my eggs. Emotionally *stable*... I mean, what was the big deal? All we were talking about was a cell, right? And how would the psychologist be able to determine whether I was emotionally stable just from merely talking to me anyway?

Pretty much right away – like Ruth had predicted – a recipient had picked me. But then, as we were about to get started, the recipient and her husband inexplicably changed their minds about using a donor; they wanted to keep trying on their own for a while longer. So Ruth and I had to wait for another couple to come along. This shouldn't take long, however, Ruth promised.

This time she was wrong; the weeks passed and nothing happened. When one and a half month had gone by I was beginning to get scared that I must be cursed, that some mysterious power had decided that I would never ever get to donate my eggs. I couldn't for the life of me figure out why all these problems arose each time *I* tried becoming a donor whereas Ilse, who hadn't even heard of egg donation before she met me, couldn't have had an easier time: Two days after dropping off her questionnaire – which had taken her over *three weeks* to fill out – she was matched and got off to a smooth start. It wasn't fair, I thought in a moment of jealousy and self-pity. How come all this was happening to me? Maybe I didn't have what it took to be picked as a donor. Maybe Russians weren't as popular as Norwegians. Or maybe I wasn't pretty enough. Thoughts like these passed through my head, as I tried to find an explanation. Ruth and I spoke on a regular basis. She told me to be patient and not to take it personally the fact that it was taking a while. It happens sometimes that even the best donor had to wait, she assured me. All I could do was to hope that Ruth was right. She better be, because I needed that money soon, having recently bought a fourteen-year-old Mazda with a comparably nice body for a thousand even – a sum that constituted about a third of my fall student allowance – now that I had finally gotten my driver's license. I had also had some headshots taken to promote myself as an actor. I know that it probably wasn't the smartest thing to have made these purchases when I wasn't sure yet I would have enough money to live on, but I felt certain something else would come up if this donation-thing happened to fall through. (And I really *did* need a car.) Furthermore, I kind of didn't mind living a life on the edge. I have always functioned the best while in that stage just before a crisis. Still, it sure was nice to hear Ruth telling me I was matched once more and asking me to come to the hospital.

As soon as we hung up, I dashed into my room where I threw on a top, the first jean cut-offs I got my hands on in the closet, and stepped into a pair of flip-flops. The timing for this call couldn't have been better since I didn't have any classes on Tuesdays: When the sharp signal of

Ilse's newly purchased cordless phone sliced through the morning still-ness, I had just been sort of lounging on our awesome couch while eating a yogurt and checking out the abundance of stations on our TV. America's extreme collection of different TV channels was yet another (albeit admit-tedly minor) reason to emigrate from Sweden – at least, it seems like that in the beginning, when you aren't used to the supply. In my native country, in 1996, we had about eight.

I grabbed my set of keys that lay on top of the counter separating the kitchen from the living room and then I ran down to the underground garage, which housed my precious "new" vehicle. Twenty minutes later, I arrived at the clinic.

"Hey, Julia," Ruth whispered and smiled wide, covering the mouth-piece of her phone when I stumbled into her little office. A nurse had brought me there the second I announced my presence at the front desk.

Ruth held up a hand for me to allow her to finish her call and then motioned for me to take a seat. I sank down on the chair next to her desk and contemplated Ruth. It had been quite a while since I had last seen her, as we only stayed in touch via telephone. She still looked the same as in our two previous meetings except for that today she was wearing her blond hair up in a little bun and her lips were no longer dressed in that loud fuchsia pink but in a more muted salmon-colored hue. Evidently, she was talking to a potential donor. I tried not to eavesdrop, but it was impossible. As she spoke, asking whether or not the girl had ever had an abortion done, I was experiencing one of those de'ja` vu moments.

About a minute later the conversation was over and Ruth looked at me, the intense blueness of her large eyes piercing me. With her hand still resting on the receiver, she spoke.

"Julia, Julia! Thank you for making it here on such short notice. How are you doin', sweetie?"

"Oh, good. Much better now that we can start finally," I said.

"I'll bet you do. Well –" she grabbed the white paper bag that sat tucked to the side on her wide desk, opened it, and peeked inside "— I have something for you." She pulled out a white paper box the size of a medium-to-large Bible and placed it on the desk before me. She paused and looked at me again.

"Did I go over where to inject and how much to inject with you the last time you were here?"

"No, we never got that far," I answered. "But I'm a little familiar with it because I've seen Ilse do it."

"Oh, OK. Gre'aaat." She opened the box and removed from it a tiny glass bottle with a white label and a metal cap. It wasn't the first time I had had the pleasure to meet one of these little jar-like things that contained the drug called Lupron; I saw one a week ago in the fridge where Ilse had placed hers. She had been injecting herself with Lupron for the last eight days. On her very first morning of daily injections, she had asked me if I could do it for her. Pushing needles into my room-mate's leg wasn't my preferred way of beginning my morning, but since I didn't want to be unhelpful, I had still said OK.

Reluctantly, I took the syringe Ilse gave me in my hand and got ready to stick it into her upper thigh. Ilse turned her head away and stared at the TV, waiting for me to conclude my assignment.

I aimed and aimed for over thirty seconds and then Ilse's head turned back. She gave me a surprised glance.

"What are you waiting for?" she asked. "Just do it!"

I returned her glance pitifully. I had realized that there was no way I would be able to push that needle into her.

"I'm sorry, Ilse, but I don't think I can do it."

She scrunched up her eyebrows.

"What do you mean 'you can't do it'? Just stick it in fast and push that orange thing!" That orange thing was the plunger you pushed to make the fluid inside the long plastic tub squirt out through the needle.

I shook my head slowly and handed the syringe back to her.

"Sorry, but I really, really don't think I can make myself do it. Is it completely impossible for you to do it on your own?"

I wasn't just pretending to be a sissy. When it came down to needles

I was the biggest scaredy cat on this planet. If I ever had any kids of my own, they would have to pick out their own finger splinters; I would *not* be able to do it.

Ilse sighed half listlessly, half mockingly, closed her eyes, and – right before me – sank the entire, third-of-an-inch long metallic spear into her rather full left upper thigh.

Ruth dug into the white bag again and fished up a long row of syringes wrapped in plastic and attached one to the other. She unhinged one of the needles from its many brothers and sisters and unwrapped it. A shiver of discomfort went through my body. Next she peeled off the metallic cover from the Lupron vial. Then, having taken a good grip of the syringe, she thrust it through the dark gray rubber layer that had appeared now that the protective metallic shield was gone.

I watched her as she – like this was something she did every other day (which, of course, she did) – pulled up the plunger, enabling the syringe to fill up with liquid. When the liquid reached the 0,1-mark on the plastic tube, she stopped pulling. Her eyes returned to me.

"OK, Julia, you want to get the Lupron all the way up to the one mark right here on the tube," she said and pointed with her finger at this very mark. "You will have to inject yourself with this amount every day at around the same time. But I'm sure you already knew that from Ilse,"

I nodded.

"You know where to do it also?"

"Yes, like here." I marked the upper areas of my thighs with my palms.

"Good girl," Ruth said. "And all the way in with the needle." She took a closer look at the syringe and its content. Then she showed it to me.

"Do you see them tiny bubbles?"

I nodded again.

"That's air that happened to come up as I retrieved the Lupron. It happens sometimes. It's not a big deal, but it's best if you don't get it into your system. To make them go away, you turn the syringe upside down and then you just flick lightly on the side of the tube." Practicing as she preached, the syringe was flipped and she flicked on it with the white-painted nails of her thumb and middle finger. As if by magic, the bubbles immediately dispersed.

"So when am I supposed to start taking the Lupron?" I asked.

"Today, as a matter of fact."

My eyes widened from joy.

"Really? So when do you think the retrieval will take place?"

Ruth looked at the big desk calendar that was taking up almost a fourth of her desk. You could tell that she was counting the days to herself.

"I think it will be somewhere around the tenth or eleventh of October, but don't quote me on that one."

"Wow! So soon? That's like only five weeks or something! I can hardly wait!" I had gotten to know Ruth so well at this point I felt safe being myself around her. There was no need for me to pretend I *wasn't* as excited or eager as I was to get this thing going. My hunch had proven to be more than correct: She was about as real a person as they come, which made me like and confide in her further. And she was well aware of the fact that the eagerness didn't stem from anything but the money. To my surprise, one day when I had gotten the urge to let her know why I was really donating, she had had no problems with my frankness – which, at times, can be quite jarring to people not used to me. I know, sweetie, she had told me instead, don't you worry about that. *Everybody* does it for the money.

"The couple that picked you can hardly wait either," Ruth said exhilarated. My high spirits had been contagious seemingly. "As soon as I told them about you and they saw your photos they decided to go with you. They hardly spent any time at all reading your profile. It's uncanny how similar you and the woman are really." That last comment was uttered as if to Ruth herself only.

"Really? That's great! But what about meeting me in person? Don't they want to meet me first?" That initial couple, the one that had canceled on us, hadn't wanted to meet me, which had been a bit strange to me, especially since Ilse had met with her couple. At the time, Ruth had explained that, in her experience, it was unusual that their clients ever wanted to meet any of the donors; the fact that Ilse's recipients had wanted to see her was a rare exception.

"No, that won't be necessary this time either. Is that awl'riight with you?"

I shrugged. "It doesn't really matter to me either way."

Following the clinic's tradition, it would turn out that I would never meet any of the parents. To this day, I don't understand why that was. Maybe they felt it was too personal; I'm not sure. It is hard to imagine when you haven't walked in their shoes. I just know that I think I would have wanted to meet the biological mother of my child.

I looked at the clock on my pager. I was supposed to meet a class-mate from my Biology class in less than an hour. We would do our home-work for tomorrow's class together.

"Is that it?" I asked.

"Yes, that's it. You just have to remember to call us the day you get your period," Ruth said and stuffed the syringes and the box with the Lupron back into the white bag.

"OK."

I stood up to get going.

"Do you want me to give you the first shot or do you want to do it on your own later when you get home?" Ruth wondered. She was holding the syringe with the Lupron sucked into it in her hand.

I grimaced and had a seat back down.

"I guess I might as well get it over with," I sighed dramatically, as I pulled up one of the legs to my rather large jeans shorts. These shorts happened to be uncharacteristically long-legged for me since during this time of my life I despised any clothing (except for tight pants) that didn't enable me to show lots of skin.

"Oh, let's not be so dramatic, Julia," Ruth said and wiped the area of my thigh that she would inject with a piece of cotton dipped in alcohol. It felt as though she was rubbing an ice cube against my skin. "It's not *that* bad. You'll see. It will be over before you know it...."

"AAAOOCHH!" My pained scream interrupted her soothing ranting. It was even *worse* than I had thought.

Quickly pulling out the needle from my thigh, Ruth placed another piece of cotton dipped in alcohol above the little stick to stop the couple of drops of blood that leaked out of it.

"Now, that wasn't so bad, was it?" she asked.

"It was *terrible*," I whined like a little kid.

"Oh, hush, Julia. I thought you were a big girl," she laughed. "And it would have hurt more if I didn't take you by surprise. By the way, when you do this yourself, don't forget to first wipe the top of the Lupron bottle before you stick the syringe into it. You have to do it each time. With these." She held up a series of prepackaged alcohol-wetted miniature napkins from the bag. "You also have to wipe the stick afterwards. Just like I did. OK?"

I nodded in docile understanding while blowing at the violated area of my thigh, as though that would take away the supposed unbearable hurt. Then I stood up. As I theatrically limped out of her office, carrying the bag of pain, Ruth laughed again and shook her head.

6

FACING THE ENEMY

Once more I walked through our apartment in hopes of finding something else that needed to be cleaned. Surely, I couldn't have taken care of everything already. That was impossible! I mean, not even half an hour had passed since I began to satisfy my sudden urge to put every square inch of our rather spacious but frugally furnished living quarters into polished perfection. No, there *had* to be more left. If I just kept looking, I would soon encounter a corner in which clusters of dust particles had gathered and somehow escaped my probing eyes; or I would spot a dirty fork hiding behind a bed that needed to be washed, or a speck in the bathroom mirror that longed to be removed. But no matter how many times I stooped, looking under furniture or scrutinizing every imaginable flat area, I couldn't see anything. Ilse's nearly daily cleanings obviously were as thorough as they were obsessive.

Utterly defeated, I sank down on the red couch in our living room. Placing my elbows on the coffee table before me, I rested my face in my hands. Oh well. I might as well give up coming up with excuses. Because, whether I liked to admit it or not, another excuse was all these past frantic twenty-eight minutes had been – and *not* to surprise Ilse by dealing with my turn to clean the apartment earlier than agreed. (Yes, despite not being what one would label a neat freak, I did do my share in the apartment. However, as Ilse insisted on cleaning all the time, the apartment never got to become really dirty.) And before I began to clean I had spent about an hour reading both the BackStage West and Dramalogue in search of independent movies or non-union commercials or plays I could audition for. (Not too long ago, I had come to the conclusion that if I was serious about giving this acting-thing a shot, I better work on getting some actual meat on my resume soon. As of yet, very little was on it.)

No, there was no more escaping what I had to do. It was time to face the enemy.

So I forced myself to acknowledge the white box that lay on the coffee table, waiting patiently to be opened. With determined fingers, I grabbed it and pulled out the tools necessary to complete the task I had spent the whole morning avoiding. Soon I was sitting with the filled syringe in my hand, ready to execute my first shot of Lupron.

But, of course, I couldn't make myself do it. I think I sat there with my beneedled hand frozen in the very same position for more than fifteen minutes before I realized this.

Come on, Julia, you can do it! I spurred myself on. It is not the end of the world. *Just stick it in!* It will only hurt for a second. No, not even that – *half* a second. Stop. Being. Such. A. *Baby!* I stared at the sharp, angry-looking thing that wielded so much power over me. Why, why, why was this so incredibly hard for me to do? It is just a little needle, for God's sake!

Closing my eyes, I took repeated deep breaths through my nostrils, hoping that this would relax my tense body and infuse me with the bravado needed to complete my assignment at last. But it seemed to have the opposite effect because I could feel sweat trickling down the side of my face. Irritated, I wiped it away with the back of my hand.

"OK, Julia," I said out loud. "Think about all the money you'll make. That should do it. Think about all those beautiful dollar bills that will fill your bank account if only you stick this damn needle into your leg." Doing my best to focus on how easy my life would become after I had managed to get the Lupron in my system, I waited and waited for a sign of the paralyzing fear within me to subside. I remained seated like this on the edge of the couch for what felt like another fifteen minutes.

Finally, I opened my eyes again. I put the needle down on the table before me and leaned back into the couch. This wasn't working. What was wrong with me? How come I was so scared of sticking this third-of-an-inch, extremely thin needle in my thigh? I couldn't figure it out. All

I knew was that trying to give it to myself was even *worse* than when I tried giving it to Ilse. It couldn't have been that painful when Ruth gave it to me, could it? I felt certain it couldn't. To further convince myself of this, I made myself relive yesterday's trying moment. As it came back to me goose bumps developed on my arms, making the hair stand straight up. And this was despite that currently it was seventy-nine degrees in our living room. Well, that approach sure wasn't the right one, I thought annoyed; now I was even *more* fearful than before. What should I do *then*? I shook my head and sighed out loud.

Wait... Wait a minute. She *did* take me by surprise...

I was filled with a wave of renewed hope. I had to take the surprise-factor into account when trying to determine the level of pain, didn't I...? Yes – I absolutely did! But I soon remembered that Ruth had claimed that, by not being aware of it, the pain was supposed to be *lessened*... Aaaaaghh! This was going nowhere.

I had about ten more minutes to waste before I had to get my butt in gear and head for school; otherwise, I would be late for class again. As of the last couple of weeks, I had gotten into the habit of arriving a few minutes late for nearly all of my classes. This was something I very much wanted to nip in the bud before it got worse.

I just had to get this damn Lupron inside my body first.

"OK, Julia," I told myself. "Let's take it from the beginning. Let's pretend you just sat down to do this. And keep in mind: IT'S NOT THAT BIG A DEAL." I rubbed my forehead for a few seconds as if that would somehow remove the past thirty minutes of failed attempts. Then I opened up another of the pre-wetted, plastic-enwrapped alcoholic swabs. Throwing the protective cover on the table, I proceeded to wipe the skin on the upper half of my thigh, the other leg this time. It felt surprisingly soothing on my hot skin, not cold and terrible like before. That was a good sign. I picked up the syringe with its glaringly orange plunger from the table and, inhaling deeply, I brought it a couple of inches above the correct area. OK, stick it in now, Julia. Don't think, just *do* it!

Again I couldn't make myself do it. I let the hand with the needle sink down onto the couch beside me.

I didn't know what to do next. If only Ilse were at home, that way she could do it for me! (She had left for school forty minutes earlier.) Oh, I guess that was just as well, though. I really didn't want to get dependent on her dispensing my shots anyway – or anyone else for that matter. That would just serve to make my life even more complicated than it already was. No, I had to learn to do it myself. And, one way or another, I *would* get this thing into my leg. Hmmm… Well, what if I, instead of plunging it into my flesh, simply tried wriggling it in? Somehow doing it in reverse… Maybe that would be easier. I doubted it, but it was worth a try.

Grabbing the top layer of meat on my thigh, I took a firm hold of it between my thumb and index fingers. And then, once more, I brought the needle-equipped hand above, albeit much closer this time. As the tip of the needle met my skin, I squeezed my fingers harder together so that the flesh would take the needle instead of the other way around. Small sticks of pain assailed me, as I could feel it enter. An acute urge to stop overwhelmed me in that moment despite that this pain was not by far as bad as when Ruth had given me the shot. Don't you *dare* stop, Julia! I told myself sharply, as the needle penetrated further; you're almost there. Filling up my insides with large quantities of calming air, which reduced the pain into nearly nothing, I forced myself to press on. I noticed then that, if I squeezed really hard and moved the needle back and forth, I was actually about to get the needle inside my leg without feeling hardly anything at all. Hey, this was *working*… Not only was I finally about to give myself this shot that had filled me with such fear last night I tossed and turned in bed two hours longer than normal before entering la-la land; on top of it, I had invented a close to pain-free way of doing it! I always knew a genius was hiding within me somewhere… Just a little more and then I would have broken through that tough, seemingly impenetrable *second* layer of skin. For some reason though, this part of the push provided more resistance than the first (and, alas, a bit more pain too, I soon came to realize). Come on, Julia; it's almost over. Push, push…

Breathe in, breathe out! Keep up those movements side to side... Push, push; it's almost in. Keep up the breathing... Once more I succeeded to breathe away the pain... I could feel how the very worst part was over; one more wiggle and it would be in...

Zzzzzzzzzz!!!!

The unexpected sound made me jump so violently I lost grip of the syringe, which of course slipped out of its hole and fell onto the floor. I stared at the little needle resting peacefully on the rug right next to my naked foot. Godammit!

Zzzzzzzzzzzzzzzz!!!!

Once more the angry sound of someone pressing our apartment buzzer by the entrance door downstairs burst through the room.

Frustrated to say the least, I stood up and walked over to the intercom. Forcing myself to sound normal, I pressed the speaker button.

"Hello?" I said.

"Julia, de ar Ilse!" Ilse's wound up voice said. "Jeg har glomt nycklerne mine . Kon du oppnu doorn?"

"What?!!" Not only had Ilse interrupted my first, highly sensitive date with the needle; she was speaking Norwegian to me, too – when she knew very well I couldn't understand it! Not bothering to ask her what the heck she was talking about, I simply pressed the "Door" button so that she could enter.

Not one minute later she stormed inside the apartment through the door that I had left open. Meanwhile, as very little time remained before I had to leave for school, I had rushed back to my place in the sofa and returned to my needle-turnings in hopes of once more finding that great, almost pain-free manner in which I had almost succeeded in executing my shot.

"Hei, Julia, hvordan ar..." Ilse began, looking beyond me with a wild look in her eyes at the same time as she started lifting every book and paper on top of the coffee table.

"Ilse, please, no more Norwegian!" I implored. "I don't understand it. What's wrong?"

"I forgot my keys. I need them to get into my locker. My math books are in there and I need them to study for the test tonight. Every minute counts because I haven't studied at all, and I have to get at least a B on this test or else I won't get any more student money from Norway. Have you seen them?"

"No", I mumbled. The idea of asking Ilse to give me my shot now that she happened to be here fleeted by me, but I quickly discarded it. Considering her upset state and the rush she apparently was in, I feared that she might be *especially* forceful while doing it. So I pressed my teeth together instead and kept rocking the needle back and forth like before. With surprising ease, it broke the first layer of skin. OK, we were back on track...

"Aoooch!!!!" I yelled, but more from surprise than from actual pain when Ilse vehemently bumped into my side while bending down to look under the couch. She straightened up swiftly and threw me a sheepish glance. "I'm so sorry, Julia! Are you all right?"

"Yeah, I'm fine," I muttered somewhat grumpily.

"What are you doin..." A big grin parted her round face suddenly, as she looked at my leg. "Oh, you're taking your Lupron... Good job! Honestly, I *never* thought you would be able to give it to yourself."

"Thanks, but it's kind of early giving me praise. I've been trying to get this damn thing into my leg the entire *morning*."

Ilse looked at me with a perplexed expression on her face.

"What are you talking about, Julia? I don't think you can get it much further in." Her eyes went down to my leg again. "And you have even pushed that orange thing all the way down." This time I, too, looked at my leg. To my utmost surprise, I discovered that she was right: The syringe I had been struggling so to get into my flesh was presently embedded deep into my thigh with the plunger pushed in.

I was stunned to say the least.

Nonetheless, it didn't take me long to figure out exactly how it had happened: Ilse bumping into me must have made me push in the needle and the plunger. And because of the pain in my shoulder and upper arm,

I hadn't noticed it entering.

I told you, didn't I? I *knew* I would do it one way or another.

7

THE SWEDISH MAFIA IS ALERTED (OR NAME-CALLING)

About three weeks later, I was standing in line by one of the two windows belonging to the Burger King located in the campus's food court. All kinds of different foods were offered in this area. Besides hamburgers, you could have Panda Express Chinese food, Taco Bell, frozen yogurt, sushi, pastries in a pastry shop, there was a hotdog and waffle stand, a soup and salad bar, a Starbucks (of course) and, last, Santa Monica College served its own homemade delicacies. Nine times out of ten though, I was a patron of Burger King's offerings, as I had developed a severe addiction to their jumbo-sized baked potatoes with sour cream, butter, and chives. And this day I definitely needed one, if not two, of those steaming brown things. See, today was the day when I would have to penetrate one of my buttocks with that monster of a syringe, the "Two-Incher", as Ilse and I had begun so lovingly to refer to it.

We had come up with that very descriptive name right around the time Ilse was due to inject herself with it. Waiting for the American History class we were both taking to start, we were standing outside the locked classroom that day. The teacher was late, so just about every other student had arrived already, too. As we were about to have our midterm exam, most of the students were quietly going over their notes or reading their textbooks. Ilse and I, however, were discussing the large needle. The coward in Ilse the Intrepid was emerging now.

"How big do you think it could be, Julia?" Ilse wondered.

"I'm not sure. Three inches maybe?" I said.

Ilse's eyes widened.

"*That* big? Jesus, I hope you're not right! I don't think I could handle it."

"Really? I thought you could handle anything," I playfully teased her. "Well, maybe it's just a two-incher."

Ilse exhaled, looking only slightly comforted.

"Yes, that's what I would think it is. It sounds more normal. Although, that's *still* pretty big," she added. A guy with curly brown hair, who had been standing right next to us all along supposedly reading something, looked at us then and shot Ilse a grateful smile.

I had been on the Lupron for a while now and, believe it or not, it was no longer such a big deal for me to push the tiny needle into my leg. It was only that first day I had found it to be so extremely terrifying; after that, slowly but surely I had gotten used to injecting myself with the stuff. (I think the powerful spell it had cast over me must have broken the second Ilse slammed into me.) It really wasn't so bad. Actually, to be completely honest, I had almost come to *like* doing it, in a twisted, masochistic sort of way – at least once in a while. It was kind of fun watching how, as I pushed the plunger, the liquid entered the subcutaneous layer above the muscle on my thigh. Sometimes the liquid didn't dissipate into my body right away, but instead seemed to get stuck right under the skin, forming a slightly larger than quarter-sized bump. This was not dangerous in any way, a nurse had explained to me, as I had called the clinic dead scared air had accidentally entered the syringe when I sucked out Lupron from the bottle, air that would now reach my heart and make me explode. I had read somewhere that this could happen if you got an air bubble into your bloodstream. But the little swelling had nothing to do with air, the nurse explained. She also let me know that even though it wasn't a good thing to get air into your blood, your heart would most likely not explode from it.

If there was one thing that bothered me with having to inject myself with the Lupron every day it was the fact that I was so good at hitting every vein on my thigh I had begun to develop some serious bruises. Soon it was easier to find a discolored patch of flesh than a skin-colored one. So I switched legs. After about a week the same thing had happened there. But, since I had always been one to bruise easily anyway, I didn't worry too much about it; I just wore – albeit reluctantly – longer shorts or skirts on the days I looked like I was the victim of some severe, odd kind of abuse.

In the midst of all this bruising Lupron-intake, I had my period. I called Ruth immediately, who made an appointment for me to come over and pick up the rest of the medication. I did so. It was in this order of drugs that the much, *much* larger syringes had arrived finally. At the sight of them, I understood immediately that even though I nowadays had developed quite the amiable relationship with my Lupron needles, it didn't in any way include these other needles.

At any rate, this time some of the miniature bottles were filled with a white powder called Perganol and the others with a light pink powder named Fertinex. These powders were different types of fertility drugs – or hormones actually – that I was supposed to mix with a bit of saline solution and then shoot up into the corner of one of my buttocks (Northeastern or Northwestern corner, depending on which buttock was in question). The reason such a large needle had to be used was because, as opposed to the Lupron, these powders had to reach further inside me. They had to get deep inside the muscle. When they were far into my buttock, they would trigger my ovaries to produce more mature eggs than the normal one. After about ten days of injecting these heavier drugs, I would be ready to – if everything went according to plan – unload a whole batch of eggs. My laying date had been scheduled only three days after Ilse's. Since her recipient's period had been delayed, forcing Ilse to hold off before she had been able to start the stimulating drugs, her retrieval date had been pushed forward, placing her almost on the same track as I.

I reached the Burger King sales window where a black girl with an intricate pattern of different-sized braids wriggling around her scalp like tiny snakes and nails so long I wondered how she managed to push the buttons on the cash register asked me what she could do for me. Deciding on one baked potato, a diet coke, and a chocolate cheesecake for dessert, I paid and got my number to pick up my food at another window.

I had the food in my hands at the exact same time – one-thirty – that I was supposed to meet Ilse. Ilse would be the one to administer this shot, like I had done on her a few days earlier. We had both concluded pretty rapidly that it was just impossible to give it to oneself.

It hadn't been easy for me to stick this large thing deep into Ilse's butt cheek. She had to plead and beg and finally order me before I eventually managed to do it. (I had to pretend she was a diabetic whose blood sugar had dipped so low that, if I didn't give her a big shot of insulin, she would die.) Then, luckily for me, the girl taking my spot as Ilse's room-mate, now that I had found a new place to live, had moved in with us yesterday, a week earlier than planned. This girl, Jessica, another Swede, had no fear whatsoever of either large or small needles, so she became the one in charge of injecting Ilse's Two-Inchers.

My rendezvous with Ilse was supposed to take place just outside the school cafeteria in front of the college bookstore, so I headed in that direction. As soon as I stepped out of the building, I spotted parts of "The Swedish Mafia". The Swedish Mafia was the name Ilse and I had given a cluster of Swedes enrolled in the college that were in the habit of hanging together whenever they got the chance and acting as though they owned the place. I spent time with them once in a while.

It was nice and warm in the large yard, a glorious day, identical to all of the other maybe 120 days I had spent in California so far.

I looked around for Ilse, but I couldn't spot her anywhere; apparently, she hadn't arrived yet. I decided to kill some time chatting with Katya and Helena, two Swedish girls I had become acquainted with recently. They were lounging lazily on one of the many long benches this area was furnished with. Along with some of these benches were tables. Both the benches and the tables were made out of some kind of yellow-painted stone.

The white-blond girls soaked in the sun while puffing on cigarettes. Tanning and smoking are probably Sweden's two most beloved pastimes. I don't think I know of any Swede who doesn't love to cover herself or himself in tanning oil and bake themselves so much they become virtually unrecognizable. Add to that a scary intake of cigarette smoke and one begins to wonder if it is possible that the now almost clichéd warnings of how frequently these two habits provoke cancer somehow have escaped Sweden. As a teenager I myself used to be an avid worshipper of treacherous UVA-rays. Often my tans were up there with George Hamilton's. Then, at about age twenty-two, when I concluded that I suffered from a deep-seated fear of aging, which ran much deeper than my fear of coming down with cancer, I vowed to never ever again let the sun get near my skin if I could help it – and if I couldn't help it I would make sure I wore a generous layer of SPF thirty sunscreen. I would rather be white than wrinkle prematurely, I said to myself. Very soon after, I had given up smoking too; at least on a regular basis. I only let myself enjoy a cigarette or two when I was partying (which, before age twenty-three, was practically every day). A year or so later, I gave it up altogether.

I took a seat on the hard sofa next to Katya, the blonder of these two peroxide-bleached blondes (yes, not *every* single person in Sweden is naturally blond). She raised a hand to shield her eyes from the sun and took a peak at who had sat down beside her. When she saw that it was I, a grin split up her makeup-free, gingerbread-colored face.

"Hey girl, how are you doing?" she said to me in Swedish, exhaling a cloud of smoke that barely escaped my face.

"Oh, good. Just fine," I answered casually. "I'm supposed to meet Ilse here."

"Who's Ilse?"

"Oh, that's my roommate."

We continued to speak about this and that for a while, though the gist of our conversation centered around Katya's new boyfriend who she seemed to be madly in love with. I was dying to let somebody else besides Ilse in on the horror that awaited my butt cheek and me. Very much unlike me I had not yet told everyone I ran into about my becoming an egg donor. Only a couple of people were aware of it, people that I had known from the first week of school, and Katya wasn't one of them. I wasn't sure exactly why I hesitated to tell her; maybe I was scared she would think I was weird or something. Which wasn't like me either. I'm not the type that worries about whether people think I'm weird or not. I just kind of do and say what I'm about and if people don't like it, it is their problem. By now, however, the way Ilse had been going on and on about how she could absolutely not tell either her parents or her friends back in Norway about her donating her eggs – and *certainly not* any of the men she would date in the future – was beginning to affect me. I had definitely become self-conscious about this whole deal. At any rate, after about fifteen minutes of how great Katya's boyfriend's abs were and how she seriously thought this was the love of her life, there was still no sign of Ilse. Where was she? Could I have told her the wrong time? I didn't think so. I was also sure I hadn't told her to meet me in front of the library where we had hooked up twice before. So where could she be? I was getting worried. My Women's Studies class would start in exactly seven minutes. If she didn't come soon, I would be late.

"So what's going on with you?" Katya wondered.

"Oh, nothing much," I said, though that wasn't true at all. Inside me, a storm of anxiety was building. The nurse had told me it was important that I took my first shot of Perganol/Fertinex before two p.m. Why it was so important I didn't know, I just knew I very much needed this egg business to work out. So where *was* Ilse? I was now looking frantically to all sides in hope of seeing her pop up somewhere. How could she do this to me, I whined to myself, when she knew how crucial this was.

"She's not showing up, huh?" Katya remarked.

I looked at her while experiencing a childlike irritation with her for putting my fear into words. No, it certainly didn't look like Ilse was planning on showing up. I was feeling desperate. Then, suddenly, my desperation overpowered my newly acquired self- consciousness: Why didn't I ask *Katya* to give me the shot? I hoped she wasn't as much of a coward as I was in terms of administering shots to people. Of course, I realized that by asking Katya to do this for me the likelihood of every person in the Swedish Mafia knowing about my business increased dramatically. But what did it really matter? What was worse when you thought about it: Being without money or risking that people thought you were a weirdo for selling your eggs? It was a simple choice. Also, I seriously doubted anybody would think I was particularly weird anyway.

"Katya," I said, looking at her pleadingly. "I need a big, big favor..."

"What? I hope you don't need to borrow money for your rent or something because I don't have a lot of money myself," Katya replied.

I smiled and shook my head.

"No, no, it has nothing to do with money. Yet. Not if you help me."

"What is it?"

Discreetly, I opened my bag and pulled out the plastic-enwrapped needle. Katya looked at me with lifted eyebrows. I could see in her eyes what went through her head. Again, I shook my head and smiled.

"No, I'm *not* a drug addict. I'm an egg donor. I have to inject some fertility drugs with this giant needle into my buttock and I can't do it on my own. Ilse was supposed to do it for me, but she doesn't seem to be coming. Please, tell me that you can do it for me! It's really, really important that I inject this stuff before two o'clock." I felt so desperate I was about to go down on my knees. But it didn't prove necessary.

"Sure, no problem, I'll do it. But why are you doing all this to yourself? That syringe looks SO painful..."

"I'll make 2,500 dollars, that's why."

That was all I needed to say to make Katya see it my way.

Like I suspected, this was the day when every Swede in school would find out I was an egg donor. But it didn't matter. Hardly anybody thought it was particularly weird, making me really irritated that I had let myself get so swept away by Ilse's nonsense. On the contrary, about ten of the Swedish women eventually decided to donate their own eggs.

Katya became the first in the long line of egg donors I referred to Ruth.

8

Laying Eggs

The day had arrived when my eggs were due to face the world. It was very early in the morning of this Monday the ninth of October, about six a.m., and most of the sun was still hiding behind the Santa Monica Mountains. As of yet, everything in the cycle had gone according to plan. The only thing that had come as a surprise to all of us had been the amount of follicles – a fancier name for clusters of eggs – I had produced. A fertility doctor tries to regulate the intake of hormones so that the donor's production of mature eggs stays around fifteen. In my case, Dr. Goldberg, my doctor, discovered during my last couple of days of Perganol and Fertinex that my ovaries were extraordinarily productive. It didn't matter that she told me to skip the last two shots (altogether I had taken eight of these injections), the mechanics of my body had still managed to become so stimulated that I just kept growing more and more follicles. During the last of the five ultrasounds I had been through, the one taking place three days earlier, Dr. Goldberg had counted to more than twenty-four eggs. She had let me look into the monitor to witness this very fascinating view for myself. I couldn't say that what I saw was all that sensational. Of course, it was the first time I had ever seen a close-up of my reproductive organs – or anybody else's for that matter – so I had nothing to compare it with. To me, instead of what it was, the insides of my uterus, it looked more like somebody had taken a shot of the star-filled sky during an unusually clear night with a camera situated two feet under water, and then inserted the photo into the machine.

What I found more incredible about my body's reaction to these fertility drugs was that, evidently, I must have gained a few pounds. See, I could no longer close the zipper to any of the tight jeans I normally wore *despite* that I had been so stressed lately with school and tests I had hardly eaten anything at all. I mean, I had thought upset, as I tried my best to close my pants one recent morning; in proportion to the few calories I had consumed the last week, I should be thin as a rail! Therefore, I was happy beyond belief to hear that the sudden increased volume of my stomach had nothing at all to do with my having gained five pounds of fat. No, the reason I had been forced to go to school that day in a pair of really ugly sweatpants was due to my retaining five pounds of *water* (thank God!). This meant I didn't have to deal with what I had become convinced was a highly depressing truth about me: My 25-year-old body had hit that wall most other women only reach at around age thirty, which is the age when a lot more of what they eat turns into fat than what they are used to.

Either way, because of this state, Dr. Goldberg told me not to teach any of the three ninety-minute high-impact aerobics classes I had begun teaching every weekend; my enlarged ovaries might not be able to handle the intense bouncing. They had grown so large in order to retain all the eggs – to about the size of two medium-sized grapefruits – that they ran the risk of twisting themselves. I really didn't feel like giving away any of these classes, but in the end I agreed to get them substituted. Although getting a substitute meant I would lose about a hundred dollars, I realized soon that I stood to lose much more if something bad happened to me. I couldn't risk that. And, more important, I wouldn't be the only one affected were something to go wrong. The recipient had hired me to perform a service; I intended to follow through on our agreement.

At any rate, there I lay on top of a crispy clean hospital bed waiting for them to roll me into the operating room. The retrieval wasn't scheduled until eight-thirty a.m. I couldn't understand why I had to be there as early as two and a half hours before. What would I be doing for so long? It would turn out it wasn't much. They were just being overly cautious. The way they saw it, I guess, was that they would rather be safe than sorry. When I had arrived ten minutes earlier (half asleep still and a bit grumpy) I had to fill out a few standard type forms stating that

I was doing the operation voluntarily, that I had no valuables with me, and that I wasn't allergic to anesthesia or had any kind of medical restrictions. They also wanted to know whether or not I was on any medication. I wasn't. Then I had to get naked and change into one of those spacious cotton robes hairdressers normally use to cover up their customers. The only difference was that here they wanted me to keep the opening on the backside. Then I had to wear a pair of thick white stockings a la Pippi Longstocking and a shower cap-resembling thing for my hair. My contacts had to be removed.

When I was dressed in my egg-laying outfit and ready to go, just one more thing remained before I could relax and begin killing time by reading every hospital-owned tabloid I could get my hands on: The nurse had to make sure my body was receiving liquids, and later the anesthesia, by hooking me up to one of those see-through IV bags – *with a big and very scary needle.* It took the poor nurse about five minutes before she succeeded in getting that sharp thing under the skin of my hand.

The drip turned out to be a good thing, as I hadn't eaten or drunken anything since before twelve a.m. last night. I wasn't hungry yet, but my mouth was getting dry. Now though, as the cool water entered my body through my hand, I could feel how the dryness slowly disappeared. It was a weird but sweet sensation.

More than an hour passed before anything else happened. I was so deep into the *National Enquirer* I was reading that I didn't notice when two young, Arab-looking men dressed in green hospital uniforms were standing next to me, ready to roll me down to the operation room. By now I was fully awake and almost enjoying my leisurely morning at the hospital. What I was about to do felt about as alien to me as the life of Michael Jackson, who I had just been reading a long feature about.

After a few long corridors and one elevator ride, we arrived just outside the end station. We stopped there a few moments so that I could make myself acquainted with the anesthesiologist, a perky man with a face as smooth as a baby's butt. He came up and shook my hand and introduced himself as Mark. Then, out of nowhere seemingly, Dr. Goldberg showed up. I hardly recognized her in her operational outfit – light green cotton pants; short-sleeved jacket; close-fitting, super-sized, yamukka-style plastic cap. All of her curly steel-gray hair was tucked in. She came up to me.

"Hi, Julia! How are you feeling? Has the stomach grown even bigger?" she asked while sporting one of her one-sided, barely-there smiles. Dr. Goldberg was one of those very serious and professional doctors that, though nice and polite, hardly ever smiled. Therefore, her playful reference to the ever-increasing girth of my midriff took me by surprise. But I soon recovered.

"Yes," I frowned. "I'm about to explode soon."

"I'm sure that won't happen," Dr. Goldberg countered. "In a few days you will be back to normal size again. Just make sure you drink lots of Gatorade." The barely-there smile grew bigger. Something in those cold green eyes seemed to warm up for once. "So. Are you ready to go and get these little things taken out?"

"I guess," was all I could say. Because, it was in that moment, for the first time since I had decided to become an egg donor I began to realize the gravity of the situation. I was about to have an actual *operation* performed inside my stomach. Sharp objects would be cutting and probing within me. What if something went wrong? It very well could. There were always slight risks involved with any kind of surgical procedure. And, from what I understood, the retrieval of the eggs was a highly intricate operation that required tremendous precision. Dr. Goldberg had explained to me that I would be put to sleep and then, in essence, she would enter through my vaginal tunnel with a long, very thin needle-like tube and continue up into my ovaries where she would suck out each egg, one by one, kind of like a vacuum cleaner sucking up pieces of soil. All in all, this shouldn't take more than about an hour. If everything went like it should, I would be waking up about two hours later while lying inside a recuperating room. *If* everything went like it should, that is. Although I definitely had faith in Dr. Goldberg's competence – in fact, Ruth had told me the medical team at the Pacific Fertility Agency ranked second best in the country – I knew that even the best could make mistakes. I sincerely hoped that today wasn't the day when Dr. Goldberg would make hers. So many things could happen. What if I wouldn't be able to have my own kids in the future? Even though I doubted I wanted any, I preferred to retain the option. Like my mother had said, I really didn't know how I would feel about that issue later in life.

But, to be honest, what scared me more than the possibility of having my reproductive organs permanently destroyed was the thought of never ever waking up again. I had heard of people this had happened to, who had been put to sleep through anesthesia and then gone into coma. They would spend the rest of their life sleeping in a bed! For the first time I wondered if the risks surrounding this egg-donation thing really were worth the money. I should have demanded more money, I remember thinking. Maybe I was an idiot, after all, agreeing to do this.

As all these thoughts fought for space inside my head, I was wheeled into the operation room. Like most OR's, everything was bright and squeaky clean. A light odor of desinfection dominated the space, together with surgical equipment. A staff of five people greeted me. They were all dressed in that same green hospital uniform Dr. Goldberg was wearing. I had to move my body from the rolling hospital bed to a chair that looked much like one of those used in gynecologists' offices. Parts of the staff began to fiddle with my legs, placing them in their assigned spaces. Mark was standing next to me suddenly.

"Hi, Julia," he said and smiled. "I'm going to add anesthesia into your drip bag. Isn't that nice, not having to get it through injection?"

His comment cracked me up, dispersing my fears a bit. I relaxed.

"*Tell* me about it!" I told him.

We kept doing small talk until I felt how the anesthesia was beginning to get to me. I was drifting off. Of course, being the person I am, I simply had to do my best *not* to let sleep happen.

That was the last thing I remembered.

9

REBEL IN A WHEELCHAIR

Like on so many other mornings I wanted to just turn around and disappear back into that world where anything could happen, where there are no rules, where you can die but still go on living. Nothing was more important than remaining there. Right at that moment I was flying over an enormous blue ocean at the same time as I was having a conversation with Ilse about whether she should go out with that hot nineteen-year-old guy who worked with her in the campus book store or if he was really too young for her. (Ilse was twenty-seven at the time.) I entered the clear water. It felt cool against my skin, pleasant. I told Ilse, Hey, why not? Go for it! He is legal and he seems to like you, too. Age is just a number. I was floating around under the water, contemplating the various colorful fishes swimming my way. They looked surprised to see me, as if I didn't belong there. This made me irritated. Suddenly it was getting very bright. Ilse was telling me how she and the nineteen-year-old had made out in the back of the bookstore and that he knew that cute black guy who worked there, too, that I liked. Another shock of brightness interfered with her tale. She told me how the young guy had told her about something the black guy had said about me. More bright interference. According to her guy my guy really thought I was... The brightness grew, effectively killing the situation with Ilse. It *demanded* attention... The black guy liked when I.... Daylight sneaked behind my closed eyes, annoying them. A winner was emerging in this subtle fight between the conscious and the unconscious, the right one. Slowly, I opened my eyes.

I had no idea where I was. Months must have gone by. Everything in this large, very bright room was so blurry. The sunlight flooding in through the tall windows was blinding despite the rather thick white linen curtains hanging before them. Second by second my eyes gained focus. Next to me, on both my sides, there were neatly made hospital beds edged by foldable steel handles. Cheap glassed-in pictures featuring sailboats in the sea and beautiful children playing in a meadow hung from the white-painted walls. A couple of random chairs were placed here and there, and there was a table by the wall. A black TV seemed to be floating in the air like a big box-shaped flying saucer before I discovered it was attached by a thin metal arm.

I still didn't know where I was; I only knew that I no longer wanted to go back to sleep. (Although I *would* have liked to know what it was that black guy in the bookstore had said about me...) I moved my arms back so that I could push myself into a sitting position. *Ohhhh...* A sudden wave of pain spread inside my stomach and I let my arms fall back down. That was all I needed. In an instant everything came back to me: the operation, egg donation, Dr. Goldberg, my life and how it had been only a few hours earlier. Even though I didn't know exactly how long I had been sleeping, I knew with my rational mind that not too much time could have passed. But it felt as if I had been out for days. So things couldn't have gone all *that* bad then, I thought. At least I was still alive and awake. Speaking of being awake, by the way, I was waking up rapidly now. I realized I was hungry, very hungry. I needed something sweet to eat – and I wanted it immediately. I wasn't sure how to get it, though, since I was alone in the room and not only was I in pain but my arm was still hooked up to that IV bag.

As I lay there turning and squirming, trying to figure out the best way to sit up while experiencing the least amount of pain, a nurse with glasses entered the room.

"Hello, Julia. Are we all awake here?" she sing-sang while approaching my bed. She stopped for a moment and contemplated me, as I tried to determine where I had seen her before. I couldn't remember her face, but since she knew my name, obviously we must have met at some point before. Even though this endeavor wasn't successful, I still managed to smile as if I couldn't be happier to see her again. I had found the answer to my woes...

"Yeah..." I confirmed. I decided to go right to the point – being in the disabled state that I was, I felt I could get away with it without appearing rude or pushy. "Euuhmm... Do you think you could get me something to eat? Some cookies or something?"

"Well, let me see what I can do. Although you're not really allowed to eat anything for a while. I really shouldn't be giving you any."

"Oh, really?" Why not? I wondered silently to myself. "What time is it?"

She took a look at her wristwatch.

"It's a quarter to ten."

"A.m.?" I realized as soon as I had said this that of course it was ten *a.m.* – unless we had suddenly relocated to Alaska during those months when the sun never sets. But the nurse didn't seem to find my question strange at all, which made me think, if only briefly, that maybe, against all reason, we actually *could be* in Alaska.

"Yes, you woke up really quickly."

"Did everything go OK?" I asked. "I mean, with the operation and everything..."

"Yes, everything went just fine. You had a whole lot of eggs there, over thirty, I think. How do your ovaries feel?"

I felt whether I could feel them. I could.

"I can feel them. A *lot*. Is that normal?"

"What? Feeling your ovaries afterwards?" She had begun to remove the tape that secured the needle of the drip to my hand.

"Having so many eggs."

"Well, it's not normal, but it's not that strange either. You just got a little hyper- stimulated. You're one fertile girl, that's for sure. You'll have lots of kids one day. Would you like me to give you something to make the pain go away?" She pulled out the needle.

"No, I'll survive." Now I knew what to do in order to get me some cookies. I would play the sympathy-card... "I only want lots of cookies.

That would make me feel better."

"I'll see what I can do." She gave me a smile and left as suddenly as she had appeared.

A few minutes later she returned. She was holding a plastic cup in her right hand and something else in her other. As she reached the bed I saw that what looked like cranberry juice was in the cup and two tiny packs of crackers in her other hand. Was that *all* she could come up with? I thought disappointed. Those small things would definitely *not* soothe my ever-growing hunger. But I didn't say anything; I just received the items in my hands and stretched my lips into what I hoped seemed like a grateful smile. She bent down and fiddled with something next to my bed. All of a sudden my upper body was moving forward, pushing me into a more upright position.

"There," the nurse said, as her head appeared next to me again. "Is that better?" I realized she was the one responsible for me sitting up.

"Much better," I answered, mouth full of graham cracker. I had never before tasted such delicious graham crackers. Very soon both packs were empty, as well as the cup, right around the time the nurse got ready to leave the room again.

"Euhhm… Excuse me," I said, as she opened the door. She turned around and looked at me.

"Yes?"

I held up the cup and shot her what I thought could be an irresistibly puppy-eyed glance. "Could I have a refill and some more crackers?"

"Oh, but Julia! You *really* shouldn't be eating anything so close after the procedure!" she reprimanded playfully, shaking her head.

"Why not?"

"You might throw up."

I looked at her with genuine surprise.

"But I have never been so little nauseated in my whole entire life!"

"Well, that could change… But OK, let me see what I can do. You have to promise me that you won't tell anybody, though, or you could get me fired."

I nodded solemnly.

A couple of minutes later she returned with a second shipping of the goods (*four* packs this time!), which I gladly devoured.

"Feeling better?" she asked and smiled.

"Mmmhhmmm!" I answered, which was the truth: I felt *much* better. A few more of those crackers were exactly what I needed. I was ready to go back to sleep now.

"OK, let's see if you can stand up then."

I gave her a dumbfounded look.

"Why?" Had she gone nuts? What was going on? Had my demands pushed her over the edge? I didn't think it could be good for me to stand up so shortly after the operation.

"Well, first of all we need to make sure you can pee. And then you will have to switch rooms, back to your old room. This is only the recovery room."

"But I don't need to pee." This wasn't entirely true; I could probably squeeze out a few drops if I had to. What I really didn't feel like doing was to stand up. Besides, I kind of liked this bed. It was very comfortable.

As if she had read my thoughts, the nurse said, "I'm sure you can squeeze out a few drops, don't you think?"

"OK," I said, feeling like a petulant three-year-old girl who had no choice but to give in to her mother's will. Preparing myself for another hit of pain, I began the somewhat complicated process of standing up. To my surprise, as I swung my legs over to one side of the bed, I discovered that my stomach didn't feel all that bad any longer. Maybe the reason that first attack of pain had felt so severe was because it was so unexpected. My feet reached the floor. As I shifted my weight from the bed to my legs and started a slow walk toward the adjacent bathroom, I could for the first time tell that something had been going down in that area between my legs. It felt as if somebody had crashed a truck in there. Everything was stiff, my legs, my arms, not to speak of my midriff; suddenly my body seemed like it had aged fifty years. My feelings must have been clearly featured on my face because the nurse looked a bit worried and asked if I were OK. I'm fine, I told her. I'm just being a drama queen.

Inside the bathroom I had a seat on the toilet and did my thing. Like both of us had forecast, there wasn't much to flush down.

"Any blood?" she wondered, as I reappeared.

I shook my head.

I was back into my first bed when Ruth showed up half an hour later. She was all smiles, big blond hair, and fuchsia-colored lipstick.

"Hiiii, Julia! Everything went just g'reaaat I heard. How are ya feelin'? You had so *many* eggs," she twittered.

"I know. I'm a freak of nature," I replied wryly.

The comment cracked up Ruth. She shook her head.

"Oh hush, you're not a freak. It just means that you're a Super Donor!"

Suddenly I saw the little plant she was holding in her hands. She extended it to me.

"This is for you. From your recipients. They are so pleased with you."

I looked at the plant for a moment and smelled its yellow and pink flowers. There was a little card attached. It read: Dear Julia, Thank you so much for everything. It was signed Your Recipients. Well, that was a nice surprise, I thought.

That was the only time a recipient would send me anything besides the check.

Ruth opened her little black leather bag and pulled out an envelope. Without a word, she handed it to me. There was something going on in her face that I couldn't quite determine. I opened the envelope and saw that it was a check. I removed it from the envelope. Then I just looked. At first I wasn't sure whether or not it was a mistake the number I was seeing before me. The check was not made out for 2,500 dollars; it was made out for 3,500.... I looked at Ruth. There was a big smile on her lips now. It was definitely not a mistake.

"I thought... I thought we said 2,500. What happened?" I asked.

"Well, for one thing the recipients were very happy with you. So happy that I managed to convince them that you deserved more money."

"Really? Thank you *so* much! I love you!" I felt how my lips stretched into a big grin. "That is truly fantastic news!"

"You're so welcome, Julia. But it really wasn't that hard to convince them."

"No? What did you tell them?"

"I told them the drugs had made you so hyper-stimulated that you would have to take a few days off teaching your classes and that you deserved to be reimbursed for those days of lost pay. Which you really should do, Julia. It's not safe for you to be bouncing around when your ovaries are soooo enlarged."

"I'll think about it," I answered ambiguously. And I *would* think about it, though, of course, both of us already knew the scale tipped over heavily in favor of my teaching the classes, ovaries enlarged or not. Unless I was in so much pain I couldn't move, I knew I would be on the floor. I would just not jump around as much as I usually did. The reason was not because I'm crazy or ignorant or even trying to make some sort of statement. I realized it wasn't completely safe for me to be jumping around quite yet, and I appreciated Ruth's concern for my well-being. But my fear of running out of money was much larger, much more imminent, than my fear of injuring myself. All my life I had been running out of money. Furthermore, because I had been involved in athletics one way or another practically since the day I learned to walk, I was convinced I could handle two enlarged ovaries fairly easy.

"Well, you'll do what you have to do. I can't do more than tell you to be careful. It's your own body and you are the only person that will get hurt."

"That's exactly right."

"OK then, I have got to get goin'," Ruth said. "I just wanted to stop by and say hiii and make sure you got the money. Do you have somebody to take you home?"

"Yes," I said. "Ilse is coming to get me."

"That's good." Ruth was standing in the doorway. "Tell her I said hi. I'll be calling you in the next few days to see how yew're doin'."

"That sounds great," I said. "Thanks so much again for getting me that extra money, by the way."

Ruth nodded, said good-bye and then disappeared.

An hour later a raven-haired nurse appeared in the doorway, declaring that Ilse had arrived to pick me up. She was waiting for me downstairs.

"Are you ready to leave?" the nurse asked.

"Yes," I told her. Perfect timing, I thought. I had just finished reading the last of the tabloids.

The nurse entered, pushing a wheelchair before her. She stopped next to my bed with it. I looked first at the brown-leathered, bewheeled thing. Then my eyes moved up to the nurse. I was thoroughly confused.

"Did you bring that for me?" I asked and pointed at the wheelchair.

"Yes. You're not allowed to walk after the operation."

I thought she was kidding, that this was some kind of practical joke the nurses were playing on me, so I glanced at her and began to laugh. But her face didn't move a muscle.

I stopped laughing.

"You're being serious?" I asked.

She nodded.

"Well, you know, I'm feeling fine. I really don't need a wheelchair," I explained. "My legs are working just fine."

"It doesn't matter. You're not allowed to walk out of this hospital. We have to take you down to the entrance by wheelchair."

I'm not sure how she did it, but somehow this nurse managed to convince me to actually take a seat in the wheelchair and *stay there* all the way down to where Ilse was standing waiting for me to take me home.

Maybe she is a hypnotist.

10

CHOKING BEER BARREL

What I was seeing in the mirror before me was one of the most terrifying sights of all my life. I'm not exaggerating. Call me shallow, call me whatever, but it really, truly was terrifying to me. I was close to tears. Why did I ever agree to do this? It was *not* worth all that money!

It was five days after the donation and my normally flat stomach was not even close to where it used to be; no, I looked as if I were six months pregnant. Not to mention that I no longer possessed a waist. And, what was even worse, today my stomach seemed even *bigger* than it had yesterday when I checked just before going to bed. Apparently, it was *still* growing. What I did have was two very full breasts to go with this deformed body. At a different time in my life, I might have liked this aspect, but not today. All those two balloons did was making me look even bigger and fatter.

An expanding midriff wasn't my only problem. What made this situation even more agonizing was the fact that all the water my body seemed determined to retain was pressing against my internal organs, like, for example, against my lungs, which made it difficult for me to breathe. It was an extremely uncomfortable feeling. Due to it, I had a hard time concentrating on most things, including deciphering any of the problems my Logics 103-teacher had given me for homework for tomorrow, something I had been struggling with when Ruth called. It wasn't the first time she had called me since the retrieval; due to my hyper-stimulation she had wanted to check in on me a little extra. We had spoken for more than fifteen minutes, which had provided me with plenty of opportunities to once more complain about my current physical state. How come she hadn't told me about this phase of the donation? This was *much* worse than having to stick that five-inch nail into my buttock every day, I told her. As it was, I was about to *die* soon from lack of oxygen. And I couldn't fit into any of my pants because my stomach was still growing; maybe it would never stop.

But instead of consoling me, Ruth merely laughed heartily at my whining, told me to relax, and to keep drinking the Gatorade. It was not all *that* bad; I just had to stop being such a little girl! Sometimes it took a little longer for the retained water to subside. It was nothing to worry about, she explained for the third time, though she did fully understand that, meanwhile, my existence might not be at its most pleasant. She promised I would be back to normal sooner than I knew it. And of course my stomach would look like it always had! Well, it certainly doesn't seem like it, I thought testily. Then she told me she had another couple interested in me as a donor. They would pay me 3,500 dollars as well. I did want to donate another time, right?

My spontaneous reaction to her unexpected question was a resounding *no*. Never again could I handle going through another ordeal like this one. Because, all in all, as I was evaluating this donation business now afterwards, lying in my bed, heavy, struggling to find a position that was somewhat endurable and that made it possible for me to inhale without feeling as if I was about to choke, to me it didn't seem worth all the money. That emotion was magnified each time I threw a glance in the mirror in hopes of finding that my beer barrel shape had begun to recede at last. (It was in those moments I concluded that the figure I used to have maybe wasn't all *that* bad...) But this was not what I told Ruth; for some reason I felt I should leave my options open.

"I don't know..." I said instead. "This whole deal was a little more complicated than what I had thought."

"Oh, Julia, Julia! Hooooney!" Ruth replied. I could tell that she was smiling. "It's *always* worst the first time! Now that the doctors know that you're so easily stimulated they won't give you as many drugs and this won't happen again. Next time it will be *sooo* much easier. I promise."

What she said made sense, but I still wasn't completely convinced.

"Well, *maybe* I could do another…"

"Oh, come on now, sweetie. You can do it! Of course you can. Ilse will do another one," she added, as if that would be the clincher.

"OK, I'll think about it," I said, mostly to get her off my back.

Interpreting my answer as an affirmative, Ruth gave up badgering me. She told me she would call in a couple of days to check on me and then we would talk some more about this new cycle. If there was anything I needed to know beforehand or if I felt acutely worse, I was always welcome to call her of course.

I hung up the shining white cordless phone I had bought yesterday with my recently acquired fortune and just lay there on top of my new queen-sized bed (a purchase made possible through Ilse's generosity with lending out money, but essentially, in extension, another one financed by my eggs) in my new apartment, pondering what Ruth had just suggested.

Almost two weeks had passed since I had moved into this one-bedroom apartment located in West Los Angeles. It was as spacious as the one Ilse and I had shared, but as opposed to that one, this apartment had a large balcony and was about 300 dollars cheaper. Sadly enough, as I had to pay the entire rent these days and not just half, it still ended up being more expensive. Even so, I craved to be on my own for a while and figured that at this point I could afford it. (See, I had managed to convince myself that the money I had just made was about ten times more than it really was.)

At any rate, the more I thought about doing a second donation, the less I wanted to do it. And I didn't get why Ruth had thought that what Ilse did would affect my decision one way or another. It was only to be expected that Ilse wanted to continue. I knew from speaking to her over the phone every other day lately that she had hardly experienced any side effects from her donation – which wasn't strange, as she hadn't been at all hyper-stimulated. Whatever swollenness was there had not been any larger than what took place during the days preceding her period. She hadn't had any breathing problems and she hadn't suffered any sort of pain at any time, not even on the day of her retrieval like I had. (The sharp pain shooting through my stomach, as I had tried sitting up in the hospital bed had come to visit me quite often during the next couple of days before finally tapering off.) Actually, she concluded one chilly late October night; she didn't feel all that different from how she usually felt. So of course she would do another donation! No, I could definitely not compare myself to Ilse. I decided then and there that I wouldn't do another. The cons far outweighed the pros.

I noticed that at the same time as I was thirsty, I needed to visit the bathroom. As of the last five days, this had become the story of my life: I drank a gallon of Gatorade only to seconds later have to pee it all out. The doctors had told me it was good for me to drink lots of this sports drink because it contained plenty of the electrolytes my system needed. Supposedly, it would help decrease the bloating whereas drinking water would have the opposite effect.

With effort, I pushed myself up to a standing position and began making my way out to the kitchen. It struck me, as I was walking with the same efficiency as an elderly, overweight, and rather stiff woman, that I didn't think I had ever felt more unattractive. I was forever grateful nobody could see my naked self in this moment.

I opened the refrigerator and discovered to my disappointment that I was out of Gatorade. How could *that* have happened? Oh, that's right... They had been out of the flavors I liked the most at the supermarket next to school yesterday, so I had decided to buy some at the one where I lived today instead. After mentally scolding myself and my persnickety ways for a few seconds, I reluctantly accepted the sad reality of having to sip a few drops of disgusting, *bloating* tap water to curb some of my thirst. Well, I tried consoling myself; at least I can look forward to not having to visit the bathroom once more in the next hour.

While I definitely had acquired the more visible side effects of a hyper-stimulated egg donor, I hadn't developed any fever or nausea – other typical side effects. I had only felt as though I would throw up during the first two days after the procedure, but not consistently. It was funny how that had worked: Simultaneously as I like a pregnant woman had craved certain foods – especially really greasy, unhealthy foods like fried Chinese food and brownies – I had experienced a strange sickness to my stomach. For me to be subjected to this sickness, though, I had to first have eaten something. And then, as I continued eating and a sudden need to vomit attacked me, I *still* felt like eating. It was weird. Either way, the sickness soon disappeared and all that was left was my yearning for fattening foods.

I threw a glance at my pager to see what time it was. It was almost eleven a.m. Today was a Tuesday, the day when I had no classes to attend. Instead, at two p.m., I had a meeting with a talent agency, a fairly good one. (It had cost me many expensive headshots in the mail before one finally showed some interest in me.) I wasn't sure if it was so smart for me to be doing this meeting in my present state, however. I had scheduled it two weeks earlier based on the idea that, five days after the removal of the eggs, surely I would be completely recovered from any possible side effects. Who could have imagined the worst stuff would take place *afterwards*? Even Dr. Goldberg had been a little surprised by the way things were shaping up; she had expected that the lion's share of my swelling would disappear in the days immediately following the retrieval. No, considering how important appearances were in the world of acting, my present elephantine state was a major indication for me to reschedule. But I didn't want to postpone the meeting; I had looked forward to this day way too much to not first try other options. I felt certain there must be *something* in my wardrobe that would sufficiently camouflage my midriff.

I went back into my bedroom where I opened my closet and began going through its contents. Finding something appropriate would not be an easy task, I soon realized, as pretty much all I owned these days were a series of skintight, rather short dresses and skirts; tiny but oh-so-flashy tops or snug sweaters; a few pants I had a hard time getting myself into while in possession of my regular figure (not to mention zipping up); jeans shorts of various lengths, though all close-fitting and not at all professional-looking; a bunch of bikinis, bathing suits, and microscopic workout/flaunt-your-body-while-walking-on-the-Venice-Beach-boardwalk gear. See, when I left D.C. for Los Angeles and two suitcases were all I was allowed to bring with me on the plane, I threw away as many cold weather clothes as I could since I had expected my new environment to be eternally warm and sunny anyway – or at least up until November. My prediction had proven correct; to this date, every day had been a perfect one to spend on the beach (which, of course, had spurred me to buy even smaller summer clothes when I felt I could afford it). Nor did I think I would have much use for the more business-like attire I had had to wear while doing my internship at a magazine, so most of those I had also left behind. Among the small number of things chosen to continue their rather meaningless existence with me as their owner were a form-fitted black jacket and a long black fairly tight skirt with buttons and a long slit in the back. These items were the only ones that might work, so I put them on. Having turned and squirmed and stared at myself in the mirror for over five minutes, I concluded that they did indeed work; they made me look stylish while also doing an awesome job in disguising my unshapely shape. And as long as I kept the jacket buttoned up in front it didn't matter that I couldn't close the skirt in the waistline. It still looked acceptable. Huh! I *knew* there would be something in there.

Happy to have found the right attire for this afternoon's meeting – which I hoped would result in me becoming the world's next superstar – I walked back into my bedroom where I kept the majority of my shoes. Going through them, I soon found the right ones: a nice pair of black open-toed ones. I bent down to pick them up. It would turn out that this was a huge mistake, as neither the jacket nor the skirt could handle the extra pressure placed on them when I leaned forward while bending my knees: The buttons holding the jacket together took off like bullets fired randomly from my stomach and a second slit appeared on my skirt about four inches above the original. (This new opening did an excellent job of showcasing my butt.) Or maybe this was really a blessing in disguise, because, considering the fact that I could only move with difficulty in this outfit, it was bound to have happened anyway. And I can just imagine how ridiculous I would have felt had it happened during the meeting… Either way, I now had no choice but to call and reschedule since there was nothing else for me to wear. I didn't know exactly *how* bad it would make me look to call so close beforehand – it was already twelve p.m. The only thing I knew was that I never EVER would donate my eggs again.

11

ENCORE UNE FOIS

looked out the window from the classroom where I sat this Wednesday in late November and discovered that it was raining. It was the first time this had happened since I had arrived in California. The uplifting sunshine and pleasant temperatures had been so consistent I had begun to almost believe the myth that there was no such thing as dreary weather in this particular part of America.

I returned my attention to the heavy-set Spanish Sociology teacher who was giving a lecture on how important people's environment is on why people become the way they become. Although sociology had always been one of my absolute favorite subjects, I had a hard time concentrating today. The reason for this was an easily identifiable one: last night, Katya and I and a few other members of the Swedish Mafia had gone out bar-hopping in Hollywood and now I was suffering the consequences – an ever-expanding hangover.

It hadn't taken long before I found that the rather sparse nightlife of the nation's capital – which nonetheless hadn't failed to impress me during the first few months of my existence on American soil – bore no comparison to that of a place like Los Angeles. In Los Angeles we had everything: glamorous movie stars, edgy musicians, and inexhaustible strings of simply unbelievably beautiful people; extravagant clubs, cool bars, and cozy lounges; the Playboy Mansion and the world famous Sky Bar; wild fiestas on the beach; flashy premieres and celebrity cocktail parties (not that we were often invited to these types of things; however, just knowing the possibility of another invitation existed was enough to excite us) fancy, star-studded restaurants; you name it and somewhere it was sure to be found. The only thing displeasing to us was California's insistence on closing her nightspots at such an offensively early hour as two a.m. (Some places even had the indecency of closing at one-thirty (!) a.m.) Anyway, all of it had to be enjoyed to its fullest extent, which was exactly what I began to do now that I had money to spend. Yesterday, these wonderful weeks of carefree living culminated in an especially lengthy session: First we met up at someone's housewarming party, then we had a couple of drinks at a chic bar in West Hollywood, then we moved on to Johnny Depp's "The Viper Room", and last we continued to feed our seemingly insatiable party spirits by driving over to the beach in Santa Monica where we consumed bottle after bottle of lukewarm beer bought at a SevenEleven on the way down. I didn't get to bed until about five a.m. As a result, since my Sociology class started at ten-fifteen this morning (and I had managed to make sure I was in time for class these days), I had received little sleep. Though I was still able to keep my eyes open and think somewhat coherently, not only was my ability to focus impaired, but I could also sense the birth of a throbbing headache some-where around my temples. Not a good sign; by four o'clock this afternoon I would be shot for sure.

Unfortunately, I had other things to worry about, more serious ones, things that had driven me to take the highly counter-productive measure producing this steadily growing hangover in the first place: When calling to check the funds of my bank account at five p.m. the day before, I had discovered there was less than 600 dollars left of my egg-donor money. The sound of the automated voice informing me of this disaster left me dismayed. It seemed perfectly implausible to me that I must have spent almost 3,000 dollars in less than six weeks. Surely, I couldn't have been all *that* wasteful! Or could I...? I knew seven hundred had gone directly to Ilse, as payment for the money she had lent me so that I could move to my new place. (The move had taken place right before I received my compensation and just after she had received hers.) I had spent a couple of hundred to print up additional copies of my headshots. (The agency that had called me in didn't prove to be as good as I had thought.) Then, the second I had regained an acceptable version of my regular figure –

which had taken nearly two entire weeks! – I bought some new clothes and embarked on my many excursions into the L.A. nightlife. I had also gotten into the habit of going to Starbucks for overpriced lattes (a couple of times a day actually) and I was eating out a lot more. And I had signed up for a rather expensive cold-reading class. That was all I could come up with. However, I soon realized that the state of my account was not so strange after all. Whether I liked to admit it or not, in comparison to my regular penny-pinching lifestyle, I had more or less thrown money around me lately.

Once more I peeked out the window and contemplated the enormous gray clouds and their soft emission of room temperature water. I didn't mind the change in weather; today in particular it seemed like the right one, feeling almost soothing. I could console myself with the fact that though my current financial situation wasn't exactly great, it wasn't time for me to have to start begging on the streets quite yet either. Other good things were that the rent for November and all other bills were taken care of already. And now I had not one, but two jobs teaching aerobics that provided me with a small but steady income. Together with what money remained from my eggs I would be able to carry on a tolerable way of life until the middle of January, which was when I would receive the next shipment of financial aid. But, naturally, there could be no continuation of the gay, unconcerned living I had come to enjoy so, not now and not next year. No, it was back to counting every cent again. At the thought of this, the sky outside appeared even more gray and dreary than before and the people walking in between classes seemed suddenly sad and pitiful. I got the feeling that it would never cease to rain. Surely, there must be a way for me to continue my new standard of living! I felt certain of this.

My thoughts wandered back to Ruth. In the past month she had called me every couple of days attempting to overturn my adamant decision to never again donate my eggs. During each of her bouts to sway me she had used a different approach. Sometimes she would be playful and cheery, others she would be serious and professional, and yet others she would be short of sounding whiny, though she had never once been unpleasant or overly pushy. And in terms of the format, her approach had taken on the predictability of a ritual: Before cutting to the chase, she would always chat with me about this and that for about five minutes, inserting her own particular brand of humor in just the right moments, spurring me to laugh.

Even though I had no intention of ever giving Ruth what she wanted, I nevertheless looked forward to her calls because she was a truly fun and interesting person, a person I could discuss all kinds of matters with, from frivolous and mundane ones to topical and intellectual subjects to serious and private situations; in short, I found her to be multi-faceted. Much to my disappointment, I experienced a difficulty in finding and befriending those kinds of people in Los Angeles. The ones I bumped into – and I'm not only talking about the ones I met while going out at night – seemed to concern themselves merely with what went on in Hollywood and how to become a celebrity. (In some instances, simply *meeting* one seemed to be enough.) How to stay eternally buff, tan, and skinny was also of much interest. It was fair to say that pretty much nobody was so down to earth, so straightforward and spoke with such frankness about things as Ruth. She was an anomaly in this world where fake, meaningless pleasantries ruled in conjunction with polite, never-ending smiles.

"…Julia? Julia? How long are you going to let the class and me wait for an answer?"

I returned my eyes from the hypnotizing motions of the rain hitting the ground and looked toward the blackboard, which was situated right where the voice had come from. Before this wall of darkest moss green, which here and there was adorned with what appeared to be white graffiti if you didn't look too closely, Elsa, the teacher, stood, holding me hostage with her glittering black eyes. The rest of the class had followed her example. I didn't have the faintest idea what question she referred to.

"I'm sorry, but I don't think I understood the question right. Could you repeat it, please?" I said, feeling very much like the spaced out recovering drunk that I was. Elsa gave me a look that I couldn't quite decipher and then she moved on to one of her more attentive students who immediately rattled out the answer. And that was all that was needed to get me to think less about which type of rare person deserved my precious friendship and more about why certain cultural factors produced certain types of people.

When this school day of self-inflicted mild pain and suffering had reached its end – a day that had ended mercifully early at two p.m. – I went over to the campus parking lot where my car was parked. I was determined to drive straight home where I could throw myself in bed.

Taking a seat in my old Mazda, I turned the key to the ignition. To my surprise – or horror might be a better word – it didn't start. I tried a couple of more times. Same thing. Well, that was just fabulous! Not only would I soon be so sick I would have a hard time moving without having to throw up, on top of it, my car was history. See, being the auto-illiterate person that I was, I felt certain the apparent electrical problem my car experienced, something that was relatively easy to fix, meant it would never run again.

I had to live with this unpleasant belief for twenty minutes before I found a person possessing basic car knowledge and a pair of jumper cables to help me jump-start the car. This person, a short Armenian guy, calmed me down, started the engine, and informed me there was a fairly easy solution to my dilemma. Most likely it was that my battery was weak. However, as I needed to let the engine run for a while to recharge it, I wouldn't know this for sure until I would try starting up the car the next time. So I sat there begging and pleading while driving home that he was right because I could certainly not afford either a new battery or a new alternator – which, he had explained, could also be the culprit.

Fifteen minutes later I parked in my apartment complex's lot. I remained in the car, staring at the gray cement wall in front of me for five minutes before I reluctantly switched off the engine. I figured, by then, enough time must have passed for the battery to be fully recharged. Now I had to find out whether the car would restart or not. Preparing myself for bad news, I turned the key. Nothing happened. Oh, well. With my luck, what had I expected? Listlessly, I tried a couple of more times. Just as I was about to give up, the Mazda made a coughing sound and the engine ignited. Thank *God*... I turned off the engine again and exited, filled with such enormous relief and bubbling happiness my brewing hang-over was momentarily vanquished.

So I was safe for now. Yet, the past stressful hour had served as a much needed reality check. I had totally forgotten about my car! It was inevitable that things would go wrong with it quite soon or that it would break down; this was the fate of used vehicles. I should have some money saved up for situations like these unless I wanted to revert to taking the dreaded snail bus everywhere again or depend on car-owning friends' mercy.

I definitely needed to make more money.

It didn't take me long to conclude that with a couple of more teaching situations or a low-paying job on campus, I wouldn't be doing much else but work and study and sleep. In comparison, risking a similar ordeal to the one I had been forced to go through due to my hyper-stimulation seemed more bearable. As a matter of fact, now, in hindsight, it didn't seem so bad. The nasty bloating, the nausea, and the difficulty to breathe I had experienced so intensely had metamorphosed into merely a vague (albeit disagreeable) memory, kind of like that evening when you had drunken a glass too many of that cheap wine and spent the remainder of the night hugging the toilet and filling it up with vile matters and promising yourself and God over and over that if only He would make disappear this horrible drunken state you had somehow entered, you would not so much as even think the word "alcohol" again. Ever. But of course, as if that gruesome barf session had just been some sort of bad dream, the next month or so you would end up at a bar with your friends, sipping on a glass of wine again. Yeah, I was sure I had been exaggerating. Ruth had been right in telling me I was acting like a baby. Really, it hadn't been all *that* bad. I felt sure of this now, especially since I knew I had a tendency to succumb to self-pity, to wallow in my own rather trivial problems more often than I should. I needed to grow up! And Ruth had even assured me hyper-stimulation wasn't likely to take place again... The more I thought about this, the more irritated I got with myself. How could I have let an opportunity to do a second egg donation slip between my fingers like that?

The moment I entered my apartment I ran over to the phone and punched in Ruth's number. Like expected, Ruth was very excited to hear that I had finally changed my mind.

"I'm *sooo* happy to hear this, Julia," she exclaimed in her usual Southern drawl. "That's *g'reaaat* news!"

The couple had not yet found a donor, she told me. Since they really wanted someone like me, chances were they would still be interested. She would call them immediately and then she would get back to me.

I smiled to myself as I hung up the phone. I was convinced I had made the right decision. The only thing irking me now, as I stood by the window in my apartment, was that I hadn't reached it sooner. Paranoia crept inside me. What if this couple would have experienced a change of heart like that first one and not wanted to use a donor after all? And then, if that would be the case, what if it would take months before Ruth would find a new match for me? What if she would *never* find another one? That would mean that, essentially, I would have lost 3,500 dollars. I would have lost it due to acting like a spoiled child about this whole donation-thing.

But it turned out that I was in luck: The couple did want me to be their donor.

Ruth let me know that I would start taking the drugs sometime in the beginning of December. As soon as they had figured out the recipient's menstrual cycle, she would give me an exact date.

My days as a serial egg donor had begun.

12

JUNKIE IN ACTION

I was at the end of my second donation when I happened to run into an article about sperm donors and egg donors while reading the newspaper. For the most part, the author, a feminist scholar, focused on the differences between the two. She devoted a lot of words on the fact that, when it came to sperm donation, the main concern was on men's health and not on their motivation to donate. And, according to her, men didn't have to go through hours of mandatory therapy to make them realize that children who biologically were half theirs would most likely result from their donations. "It's as if women are more emotionally connected to their eggs than men to their sperm," she concluded.

I read that last sentence once more to make sure I had understood it correctly. I had indeed. My heart beat faster and I could feel how the blood in my veins got hotter. So this was why we had to go see a psychologist... I *knew* there was something weird about it. Those bastards... (At this time of my life, I was about to enter my fundamentalist feminist stage; therefore, the writing particularly incensed me.) Well, I certainly wasn't any more connected to my eggs than men to their sperm! Absolutely. *Not!* Now I *really* didn't want to go see that psychologist I so far had managed to avoid. If Ruth brought it up again, I would make this abundantly clear to her. Thank God I came across this article!

Still irritated, I put the paper away and began to quickly remove my workout clothes so that I could take a shower and get ready for the evening. I realized I was running late; it was only about an hour left before the sign-up for stand-up comics would start at the little bar in Encino – a city located about ten miles away from my apartment. If I was going to get a spot to perform at the open mike there, I had to hurry up. See, just a couple of months earlier, I had decided that my road to stardom wasn't complete unless I incorporated stand-up comedy into it; hence, I signed up for a comedy workshop. As it turned out, at the completion of our six-week course that culminated in a performance at the Improv, one of Los Angeles's three main comedy clubs, I was one of the only two students receiving a standing ovation from the audience. From that moment on, I felt certain I had found my true calling in life: I was to be a stand-up comic!

As my pants came off and I made a mental note to later on write material regarding being an egg donor, I realized I had forgotten to take my daily shot of Lupron. Usually, I shot up between one and two p.m. and it was already four o'clock in the afternoon. This time, however, the discovery didn't faze me since I had found out from Dr. Goldberg that taking the shot at the exact same time every day wasn't quite as important as I had first thought; as long as I took it within the same half of the day, it didn't really matter. I spent a precious minute debating whether I should take it now or if it would be more time-efficient to take it while in my car, as surely I would be stuck in a minor traffic jam at some point on the road. I had yet to drive on the 405 Freeway during rush hour without having to stop on various occasions. I quickly determined that doing it in the car was the better alternative.

I left the bedroom and ran into the bathroom. It didn't surprise me much when, upon entrance, I discovered two cockroaches chasing each other in one of the corners. Nor did I find it particularly strange that there was no warm water available. I had gotten so used to these kinds of scenarios taking place more or less every day in my apartment that they didn't even upset me anymore.

Even though within a couple of days of having moved to my new place I suspected it was a bit more run down and less well maintained than the one I used to share with Ilse, it hadn't worried me too much; a certain amount of dumpiness was to be expected for such a cheap rent. And, as it was, the stains in the ceiling could always be painted over and the managers had promised the old carpet would be changed in a month or two. However, as the weeks went by, I discovered it was more than a *bit* run-down. I had my own ant farm residing in one of the kitchen cabinets and there was mildew everywhere. The heater didn't work properly, nor did the toilet; it was backed up nearly every day. I also realized that the apartment complex was managed by two alcoholics who thought it was a lot more fun to down a quart of Dewar's and a twelve-pack of Budweiser every day (*each!*) than to busy themselves with making sure their building was in an acceptable condition. (No new carpet would ever arrive.) And it wasn't just the managers who seemed to have been extracted from one of Quentin Tarantino's movies; a whole band of interesting characters shared *Casa Bonita* – the name of the complex – with me. For example, on the same floor, a few doors away from me, two transvestites housed – one tiny Asian man and a huge African-American man. I'm pretty sure they made their living from hooking. The way their schedules ran and the fact that they were always dressed in insanely slutty outfits when they departed indicated this: Every night they left together at about eight p.m. to return around four a.m. (I know this as I'm a light sleeper and they weren't exactly quiet when they passed outside my apartment.) On the other side of me, we had the obligatory bachelor living in a cigarette-stinking studio. I think he might have had a thing for me – or maybe he just hoped my evident Swedish nationality would entail more than a difficulty with pronouncing *th*-sounds and speaking with a lilting inflection – because he banged on my front door every night to see if I had some eggs or salt to lend him. I usually didn't since I only ate ready-made food such as TV-dinners and canned soups in my house and therefore didn't need it. When he got that, he stopped asking for any condiments and simply came over for "a little chat", as he put it. I felt so sorry for him I often obliged, spending a considerable amount of time on the walkway, outside our apartments, babbling and babbling about nothing. When I found out he wasn't really a bachelor, but had a Filipino wife and kid tucked away somewhere, I drastically cut down on my charity chats. Then, finally, right above me, a gang kept their headquarters. This posse of Latin anti-lovers had on more than one occasion settled their differences with loud fistfights, waking me in the middle of the night.

All right, back to the present moment: Braving the icy water, I jumped inside the shower and swiftly rinsed myself off. A minute later I stepped out, dried my body, and threw on some clothes and makeup. It didn't take me long before I had dashed out of my apartment, having made sure my box jam-packed with syringes, alcoholic swabs, and Lupron was safely tucked into my bag.

Like I had thought, within minutes of having entered the 405, I was stuck in traffic. Great, I thought while staring into the large butt of a U-haul truck through the front window of my immobile car, the perfect opportunity to take care of business. Digging into my big handbag, I pulled out the box and very soon I had the necessary paraphernalia in my hands. I knew the cars could start moving at anytime, so I had to act fast. With the hot, descending sun beating down on me through the window by my left shoulder, I swiftly removed the protective wrapping from the syringe with the help of my teeth. I shoved it through the dark gray rubber top of the little glass bottle containing the Lupron without having bothered to wipe off the top first and then I pulled out the plunger. The transparent liquid rushed up into the slim tube. Feeling like a true professional, I let go right as the liquid hit the 0,1 mark. If only Ruth could have seen me now, she would have been so proud of me, I thought as I threw the bottle back into the box I had placed on the passenger seat. And with that, we had arrived at the second step, the wipe-the-thigh-step. Not knowing where else to put the syringe, I put it into my mouth, securing it tightly between my teeth like a pirate biting his knife. Luckily, I was wearing a skirt, so all I had to do to access my upper thigh was to pull it up close to my crotch. I sighed at the sight of my bruised flesh. Some of those dark purple, huge things looked *really* scary... Oh, well. Holding on to the steering wheel with my one hand, I buried my other into the box in search of an alcoholic swab. I pulled out a row of the pre-packaged serviettes and brought it close to my other hand so that I could use that to tear off a serviette and then open it, all the while making sure I kept one eye on the road. Getting rid of the serviette's foil wrapping, I proceeded to wipe the area about to be penetrated. Great, almost there, just a couple of more steps and it is all done... I removed the needle from my mouth, hoping there were no air bubbles in it so that I could just go ahead and shoot up. But of course, I wasn't that lucky; today there were even *more* bubbles than normal floating around inside that narrow tube. I threw a quick glance at the truck before me. It still appeared determined to stay in that very same spot; however, I knew this was bound to change any second now. Rapidly, I turned the needle upside down while letting go off the steering wheel and then I began to flick at the syringe. To my utmost surprise, the bubbles disappeared on the two first flicks. I relaxed and got a hold of the wheel again.

Now only the fun part remained, the one that entailed getting the drug into my body. Like previously stated, I had come to almost savor this step of the process (though I had yet to reach the point where I applied the same ferociousness as Ilse while pushing the needle into my flesh), so before long I had managed to get the tip deep enough into my leg. Considering my pressing circumstances, I decided I better skip pulling the plunger up a bit to ascertain I hadn't hit a blood vessel; normally, as apparently I had a tendency to run into just about *every* vessel my thighs possessed, I at least tried to check. So I pressed the plunger right away instead, experiencing the strangely pleasurable sensation of how the cold liquid swam into my system. Satisfied to have completed my task with such efficiency, I removed the syringe and placed it into the plastic bag in the box where I kept all my used syringes, as nurse Monica had made it very clear to me that I should bring back all of them to the hospital.

I don't know what it was that prompted me to look out the window to my right – maybe I actually *felt* their gawking eyes – in any case, this is what I did. And when I did, I met the aghast faces of three people staring at me hard: one middle-aged man and what could easily be his wife, and their teenage daughter. These were seated in a beige Lexus that was stuck right next to mine in the traffic jam. From the size of their gaping eyes and the expression in them, I immediately understood what they must be thinking. But before I got a chance to wave dismissively and lift the box up from its hiding place so that they could see for themselves exactly what it was that I had just finished injecting, they had looked away, apparently embarrassed to have been caught. And then – of course! – merely seconds after this rather disturbing moment in time, the cars started moving again.

Feeling my cheeks heating up, I put the transmission in drive and pressed the gas pedal. As I continued driving into the dazzling California sunset, I sincerely hoped that this would be the one and only time someone thought that, by witnessing me taking my Lupron, they had witnessed a junkie in action...

13

THE MAN IN THE TOILET

In my life as an egg donor I made two close male friends. The first one I met while pursuing stand-up comedy and his name was Peter Beck. Peter, a man seventeen years my senior, was a true child of Hollywood. He was one of the many who had left a little mid-western village in America – or village in a whole other country for that matter – after college for the fame and fortune that awaited them in Los Angeles. Alas, in just about all cases, the fame and fortune rarely happened, at least not quickly. So, as they kept struggling, determined to reach their goals, they had to make a living as best they could. Peter paid his bills by writing plays for children and ghostwriting scripts for people with a great idea but no clue as to how to write it. Apart from being a gifted and prolific writer, he was an amazing stand-up comic and actor. Seeing him in action both on stage and on tape as he played a villain on *The Young and the Restless*, the highlight so far in his career, I became even more inspired to try making it in Hollywood. But let's talk more about him later. Now, let's move on to the second, namely, Jake.

I met Jake shortly after I began working as a personal trainer at one of Los Angeles's many health clubs, a job I acquired easily now that I had won a green card in the yearly green card lottery. (Yes, I know; the day I found out I had won was *truly* memorable!)

The day we befriended each other, he was standing behind the counter of his open-air fitness shop located in a corner on the second floor of the club. I had seen him various times before while training my clients and even purchased water and the occasional protein bar from him. However, we had never exchanged much other than a nod and things like: "What's up? – Fine." and "How are things? – Great." I didn't even know his name. Today as I came up the stairs and spotted him and his assistant I wish we had spoken some more. I was in the final stages of my third donation and needed someone to help me with the Two-Incher. I had tried giving it to myself for more than twenty minutes in one of the toilet stalls in the women's locker room but without success. (Believe it or not, I had actually made myself perform this incredibly masochistic act a *couple* of times prior when I had no one around to help me.) But no matter how much I wriggled and fixed, I just couldn't make myself do it this morning. So I decided I would find someone in the gym that could do it for me. Unfortunately, this proved easier said than done since the gym was as good as empty except for the cleaning lady and the gym's sales people and receptionist, and I had never before seen any of the three obviously gay men or the young Asian couple presently using the facilities' weight room. I briefly contemplated driving over to Peter, who I knew was at home and have him administer the shot, but I quickly discarded this solution, as it meant having to drive all the way to Santa Monica and back. A drive like that from where I was at the moment would take more than an hour probably – not feasible considering that my next client was due in half an hour. No, it *had* to be someone in the gym. I positioned myself on the floor in the stretching area while throwing longing glances at the stairs, hoping to see a more familiar soul ascending. Who would be the better one to approach among the staff? Who was most likely not to be freaked out by either the fact that I was an egg donor and/or the humongous syringe with which they had to give me my hormones? Having started working there just a few weeks earlier, I knew no one particularly well. It was a tough call; frankly, I didn't think any of the sales guys or the receptionist or the cleaning lady would be the right one. For some reason, my eyes repeatedly returned to the stone-faced, light-skinned black man who, a few yards away from me, busied himself with doing inventory.

Before I had time to rethink my decision, I was standing in front of his counter, looking straight at him. He immediately noticed my presence and straightened up his previously bent body.

"Can I help you?" he asked in a pleasant tone.

I smiled hesitantly for a few moments before finally speaking, "Yes, I think you *can…*"

A couple of minutes later the two of us were standing in the rather spacious handicap toilet stall in the women's locker room, first having made sure no one had seen us enter together, as this easily could have been misconstrued that we were about to do something entirely different.

I looked at the quiet man in front of me and said, "All right, let's get this over with." Pulling out the already prepared Two-Incher from the box that I carried in my sports bag, I handed it to him to hold. Much like I had suspected, the sight of it didn't make him balk at the least, just like it hadn't fazed him or made him disgusted when I told him I was an egg donor; he just took it and waited for my next instruction. This was indeed the right person…

My hands free, I stuck one of them back into the box and soon got a hold of an alcoholic swab. Quickly, I removed its protective foil wrapping. Now all we had to do was to get the hormones inside me. But as I was about to lower the waistline of my black cotton tights so that I could wipe the area about to be injected, it suddenly struck me that, when I had done this, a strange man was to get full view of the upper half of my right buttock. Was that such a good idea…? I shot a look at the muscular, wide-shouldered person next to me who stoically waited for me to finish my doings. His face was unmoved, but a certain something in his eyes – kindness, understanding – made me realize I was in safe hands. So I proceeded.

"OK," I said quietly, pointing toward the freshly wiped area on my upper cheek. "This is where you'll have to stick it in. It's enough if you get half of the needle in before you push the plunger. You'll have to make sure you push the plunger *all* the way in though. And when it's done, you can put one of these napkins above the hole," I added, taking special care to speak with the lowest voice possible (I wasn't completely sure we were still alone in the locker room) while handing him an already undressed serviette. The man nodded and then, following my example, he said very softly:

"All right. Let me know when you're ready."

Looking away, I inhaled as deeply as I could a couple of times while praying he would be less violent than Ilse yet not as hesitant as Katya, a fairly regular executor of my Two-Inchers these days.

"OK, ready!"

Hardly did I have time to press my teeth together firmly like I always did while receiving this shot, as I had noticed this action minimized the pain, before I felt the tip of the big needle breaking my skin and entering my flesh deep. A second later I could feel how the plunger was moved in to the very end of the tub. Then the syringe was removed and another alcoholic swab was pressed against the skin.

Pleasantly surprised at the smoothness with which the shot had been administered, I turned around. There was a small but content grin on the serious man's face now.

"That's it, right?" he asked, extending the syringe for me to take.

"Yes, that's it," I replied and smiled back while taking the syringe and putting it in my bag. "You were pretty good at that. Thanks so much for sneaking in here and helping me, by the way! I owe you *big* time."

"No problem, I'm glad to be of help. But, of course, feel free to pitch any of the items in my shop to your clients." The small grin grew a bit bigger.

"I'll definitely do that," I promised. "As a matter of fact, I have one coming any minute now that I think could benefit a lot from that protein drink mix you're selling. I'll bring him over after the session."

"Sounds great." He paused briefly. "Well, let's see if we can get out of here now without anyone catching us."

"Oh yes, right!" I walked to the door of the stall and listened to see if I could hear any sound of someone having entered recently. It was completely quiet. "It doesn't seem like there is anyone in the locker room still, but I'll go out first just in case and make sure – and then you can leave."

I unlocked the door and sneaked out. Like I had thought, we were alone in the locker room. As I was about to call the man in the toilet to let him know the coast was clear, I realized I had yet to learn his name. I dashed back to the stall to get his attention. He was standing right next to the door. I signaled for him to come, which he did. Right as he was about to pass me, however, I stopped him and stretched out my hand.

"I don't think we know each other's names. I'm Julia."

"Jake," he said and shook my hand. From that day on, a close friendship began to develop.

•••

So I was about to finish my third egg donation very soon, or three days later to be exact. To my utmost delight, cycle number two had gone by, just like Ruth had assured me, with hardly any of those ghastly side effects that had occurred during the initial one. I had only experienced some bloating due to a very slight hyper-stimulation; comparatively though, it had been nothing and five days after the retrieval my body was back to normal. I had even been able to teach every one of the approximately ten aerobics classes per week I taught these days. (Well, of course, the two classes immediately before it was time for me to hatch, I had made sure I jumped *very* carefully.) When Ruth called and asked if I felt like doing a third donation, which would begin only a couple of months later, it wasn't difficult for her to extract an enthusiastic yes from me. Sign me up! How could I *not* continue? Clearly, that first time had been an aberration of how an egg donation was supposed to end, which had fooled me into believing that this process was a lot harder than it really was. And now, as we were approaching the grand finale of this third one, it seemed the doctors might have figured out finally how to properly medicate my body so as not to induce even a minor hyper-stimulation because my breasts remained the same size as always and my stomach had yet to expand. (During the two earlier ones, these physical changes had begun to develop about five days before it was time for the operation.) Yes, I had definitely overreacted that first time. Thank God I had Ruth to set my head straight! The more I spoke to her, the more I liked her, and every month our relationship grew stronger. Being a lot older and more experienced than I, she had become a sort of mother figure to me – a relative – something I very much needed as I was far away from my closest friends and family in Sweden. She was the anchor in my scattered L.A. life. I no longer socialized with Ilse, which was to be expected since it rather quickly became clear we didn't have much in common. Instead, I hung out more frequently with certain members of the Swedish Mafia, Katya and her roommate being some of these, and other random Swedes whom I ran into here and there. Then there were the various characters I befriended while doing stand-up comedy – I spent many unforgettable nights with these – and the people I met in my acting classes and at the gyms where I was working. Unfortunately, the vast majority of these would prove to be only transient friends of mine, including Katya, despite that, with some of them – Peter being the best example – I did grow very close.

14

THE SUPER DONOR

"**R**eally?" I said to Katya over the phone. "I do *not* agree. He looks way too *nice*."

"He *does* not!" Katya countered. "He's super sexy. Much more than that other almost *bald* one."

"He's not bald! Besides, it's his face that makes him so sexy anyway, his *eyes* especially!"

Katya and I had been on the phone for over half an hour this evening, wildly discussing which doctor was the most sexually appealing out of the two male doctors among the Pacific Fertility Agency. I wasn't sure who had brought up the subject; all I knew was that we disagreed hotly and profoundly. The funny thing is that, a couple of years later, I would actually agree that her pick, Dr. Nixon, was the more attractive one; however, right in this moment, I couldn't come up with enough reasons as to why he was a lot *less* appealing. First of all, he was a little too built for my taste – and short, on top of this. Not a good combination. His body reminded me of that of a bulldog, stubby arms and legs attached to a compact midsection (though he was not at all fat). Then he had one of those wide necks I absolutely could not handle. Nor did I fancy his thick helmet of salt and pepper hair. What he did possess in his favor was a rather good-looking face that contained beautiful brown puppy eyes and a nice smile. Furthermore, he had a deep musky voice that he liked to use often. When he spoke he sounded exactly like President Clinton (who, and I don't care what you say now, is *very* sexy). As a matter of fact, it was like he then, if only briefly, *turned in* to the President... at least if he sat down so you didn't notice his height and I was looking at him from a distance (like when I peeked at him from in between my feet, as I lay spread-eagled in that horren-dously awkward gynecologist's chair). And, as opposed to Dr. Franzen, he seemed to have a very sweet yet manly personality – which also spoke loudly in his favor, of course.

Dr. Franzen, my favorite, was tall and handsome. He had the type of body I preferred on men: lanky but strong, built yet slim, with narrow hips and good shoulders. As Katya had pointed out already, he was on the edge of losing a good part of his dark straight hair. This seemed a bit premature, as he couldn't be more than at the most forty years old. Not that it mattered to me; I found that this prelude to bald-ness only made him more attractive. And it drew more of the beholder's attention to his, in my opinion but not Katya's, exquisite face. I thought he possessed classic good looks: a wide mouth, a slender and straight nose, a well-defined jawbone and high cheekbones. His most striking feature, however, was his deep-set black eyes that seemed to tell you things his mouth never would. Then again, as it was, his mouth never said much of anything. See, Dr. Franzen was one of those extremely, to the point of almost embarrassingly quiet people. While this could be a bit intimidating (like when you were alone with him in the exam-ination room) I thought it also added to his sex appeal, kind of like Charles Manson must have appealed to all those young girls that joined his cult.

I think the biggest reason Dr. Franzen appealed so intensely to me and me only – because most of the other girls I had discussed these doctors with were on Katya's side – was because he reminded me so much of my first serious boyfriend (who curiously enough was the one I had become pregnant with. At the time I believed that since both of them in one way or another were involved with my fertility, there just *had* to be some higher meaning attached to it). At any rate, unable to come to a unanimous decision regarding this matter, Katya and I amicably changed the subject and eventually made plans to meet up for a coffee and a sand-wich the following day.

Over two years had passed since I had settled in California, and I had recently concluded my fifth donation. I felt like the smartest woman in the world to be doing this. I was *so* happy I had discovered egg donation. The fact that I now made double the amount – $5,000 – from what I had originally been offered only added to my excitement. (This increased compensation came into effect, as I was about to embark on my fourth donation.) Gone were my constant preoccupations with money, as the income I derived from my eggs together with what I made on my fitness jobs, made me feel as if I were rich all of a sudden even though I no longer received any financial aid. If there was something I wanted or needed, I just got it without thinking twice; it wasn't like I couldn't afford it. Experiencing this was something entirely new to me and, of course, I absolutely loved it. These days, the occasions were rare that I went to the supermarket to buy food for my house; instead, I bought take-out meals or went to restaurants. I went shopping for new clothes and shoes every other week. One of my best friends lives in Buenos Aires; I went there for a three-week vacation over Christmas. I went to Miami twice for the weekend and to Vegas, too. I could use some furniture for the new studio apartment I had left Casa Bonita for, so I bought some. Naturally, I soon traded up to a better car. Also, a good part of the money went to support my desire to become a working actor and comic, as this is not an inexpensive endeavor. In short, life was pretty good.

Much like Ruth had expected when we first met, it was very easy to match me. Not only did I possess health and apparent intelligence, with my five feet eight inches and well-built body I was also considered tall and athletic. These were qualities recipients looked for in a donor (despite that some of them didn't have them themselves). Furthermore, with five successful donations under my belt – during which I had always produced more than the expected amount of fertile eggs – by now I sported an excellent track record. This was an important factor because in-vitro fertilization is an expensive treatment and the way most recipients saw it was, Why take a risk with someone who might not produce what you want? Then, of course, having gained a reputation of being so reliable in terms of never even wanting to *consider* terminating a cycle – something the donor has a right to do up until the day before retrieval – I appeared almost apathetic, didn't exactly worsen my popularity. In essence, I was turning into a sort of super donor.

For a long time there was just one minor – but, to me, profoundly terrifying – moment of possible disruption to this great collaboration of ours. It would take place a few weeks after my fifth donation was completed.

"But why are we only allowed to donate *four* times?" I almost yelled over the phone to poor Ruth, who simply happened to be the messenger of this nonsensical rule of which I had just been informed. "That doesn't make any sense at all!" I shook my head and rolled my eyes, still trying to fully digest the fact that the Pacific Fertility Agency only allowed women to donate four times each. "Especially not since sperm donors are allowed to donate *hundreds* of times each!" I added with acid, distinctly remembering the fiery writings of the scholar in that article I had read a year earlier.

"I know, Julia, I know," Ruth replied in a soothing voice. "It's absolutely absurd. Really, they shouldn't be able to set such arbitrary rules, but they can, so they do."

"But why? I don't understand the reasoning *behind* it."

"Neither do I. Actually, it's mostly Dr. Goldberg who's behind it; she was the one who created it. She finds it unethical to use a donor more than four times. I don't know how come she feels that way because, frankly, what's so unethical about it? But that's how she feels and there isn't much we can do about it. The other doctors at PFA don't agree with her and that's why they let you slip by for a fifth. But they can't allow you to do any more now; after all, Dr. Goldberg is a senior partner. Her opinion matters a lot and it would be disrespectful to push it any further."

I processed what Ruth had just said for a couple of seconds and, suddenly, memories from the last cycle came back to me. With burning clarity, I remembered how I had felt like Dr. Goldberg had looked at me strangely the few times we happened to run into each other, as I had gone to the hospital to draw blood or for an ultrasound. At the time, I was sure I had imagined the weird looks she gave me. Apparently though, I hadn't... As a matter of fact, here we had the actual reason Ruth had told me not to talk about how many times I had donated to anyone at the hospital – and especially not to Dr. Goldberg.

Especially *not* to Dr. Goldberg, Julia...

"Uh huh. That really sucks," I said finally.

"It sure does."

So *this* was why Ruth had called me today then – and *not* to let me know about yet another couple eagerly awaiting the arrival of my eggs like I had first thought when I heard her voice upon answering the phone. Disappointment mixed with an ever-growing measure of horror enveloped me at this realization. So this was it then... The end of an era had arrived, a brief but very lucrative and carefree era indeed... Having to face it so soon was really sad, truly a shame, but expected, as this thing Ruth and I had going together had been too good to be true from the beginning. Nothing this great could last for very long, not with my luck. "Oh well, it was good for as long as it lasted, that's for sure," I mused, as I reluctantly tried to reconcile myself with this new, uncomfortable reality. "But God do I wish that I could continue!"

"What do yew mean, Julia?" Ruth asked. "Well, why on earth wouldn't you be able to continue?"

What kind of strange question was *that* now? Didn't she just tell me that I wasn't allowed to...

"There are more agencies in California than PFA, Julia. PFA is only one among many egg donor agencies here. And there are other hospitals that perform egg donations. Trust me, I have lots of contacts in this world. Let's be thankful for that. You can continue donating through any of these venues; I can help you do that. Because, I have to say, it sure would be a real disgrace if you would have to stop just yet now that there are so many that want to buy your eggs – and particularly since I have a feeling that it won't be hard for me to negotiate even *mooore* money for you... Anyway, I have already told my friend over in Glendale about you and she told me there is this couple that would just *looove* to use you as their donor. That is, if *you* want to, of course..."

"When can you set up an appointment for me to meet the doctor there?"

When I hung up the phone after having received all the details for my sixth donation, I was ecstatic. Ruth was *truly* incredible! Of course there were plenty of *other* outlets through which I could donate... I laughed out loud while taking a seat on my bed. She only turned out to be more and more ingenious every week. I was so grateful she had become part of my life. Imagine if I hadn't happened to find her phone number in Backstage West that one glorious day in July. Who knows what would have happened to me without her? Probably, I would just have had to go back to Sweden... Well, let's not think negative thoughts about what could have been; let's focus on what is instead, on all the good things: Here I was in America exactly like I had always wanted, twenty-seven years old, with sufficient amounts of money at last (and more coming), soaking up the ever-present sun and the exotic surroundings, well on my way to becoming a big star. Surely, this was to happen well within the foreseeable future. Even though I had yet to find a really good theatrical agent, I think it was still fair to say that I was pretty happening; as it was, I did have one kind of agent – I had an agent for my eggs! At the thought of this, I began to giggle again. Now how many actresses could say *that*...

Of course, I wasn't much looking forward to having to travel over an hour to and over an hour back in order to continue donating (and this was when traffic was *light*), something I would have to do as Glendale, one of the many cities constituting greater Los Angeles and in which my new hospital was located, was far away from where I lived. From now on, I would have to get used to getting up *a lot* earlier in the mornings so that my blood could be sampled and my ovaries monitored by the doctors there. Still, with regard to what my life would have been like if Ruth hadn't bothered to search out this solution for me, it was really a minor price to pay. And all I had to do in exchange for this immense favor was to make sure I didn't let the doctor over in Glendale know just how many donations I had done already – that way I wouldn't face any problems, she had explained.

15

MEETING THE POT PSYCHOLOGIST

"**O**h, hush, Julia, it *won't* be that bad," Ruth admonished me as I stood before her in her tiny office, ready to leave. I had just performed my usual whining monologue as to why it was absolutely unnecessary for me to visit a psychologist, something I did each time the issue was brought up.

"You really have to do it or the doctor over in Glendale won't let you donate," continued Ruth. "She just isn't as lenient as the ones of the PFA. Besides, I have dodged this requirement for much too long as it is. You'll see how y'all will get along just fine."

"OK, OK," I finally gave in and had a seat back on the little chair next to her cluttered desk. "I'll go if it's so incredibly important. When do you want me to go?"

Ruth opened her green appointment book and scanned a couple of the pages for a brief moment. Her striking blue eyes returned to me.

"How's tomorrow afternoon for you?"

I tried to remember what my schedule would look like the follow-ing day. In the morning I had my acting class between ten-fifteen and twelve-twenty at Santa Monica College; this one plus another acting class were the only classes I took there nowadays, as my original ambition to become a journalist had become entirely overshadowed by my wish to conquer the world of entertainment. And even though I was at the point of being able to assemble enough credits among all the different college-level courses I had taken not only in my country and the U.S. but also while studying Spanish in Madrid to complete something along the lines of a Liberal Arts degree, I had lost all motivation. What did it matter if I had a bona fide American college degree if I wasn't going to use it?

Nobody cared about those kinds of things in Hollywood. Then, after my acting class, much later in the day, Peter and I were shooting an episode of his talk show on public access; he was the host and I was to appear as his exotic guest from Sweden. Well, I guess I could squeeze in a date with the psychologist between my class and Peter…

"I'm free between twelve-thirty and five," I said.

Again Ruth threw a glance in her green book.

"Two p.m. How'd that be for ya?"

"Good, I guess. Where is it?"

Ruth grabbed a pen and scribbled down something on a piece of paper.

"Do you have a Thomas Brothers' Guide?" she asked.

I nodded.

"Dr. Marit Webster lives down in the Valley. She works out of her house. I've written down her address and phone number here for you. I've been there. It's not that hard to find. And you can always call her if you get lost."

"OK," I nodded. And with that, I grabbed my white paper bag with the Lupron for my sixth donation, the original reason for my visit today. Then we said good-bye.

▼▼▼

The next day at around one in the afternoon, I sat in my turquoise and black Mitsubishi Eclipse, driving over the hills that separated Los Angeles from the San Fernando Valley, which is also known as just "The Valley".

This particular day was one of those burning August days during which it could get well over a hundred degrees in certain parts of the Los Angeles metropolitan area. If you had a working air conditioner in your car, this wasn't so bad. I didn't, however, and since I lived in West Los Angeles where it rarely got this unbearably hot, I always kept postponing fixing it. Right in this moment, with the sweat pouring in fierce strides along the sides of my face and body, I cursed myself over and over for being such an oblivious carpe diem person and not ever planning ahead.

The Mitsubishi was the fourth car in my possession in little less than two and a half years. I had bought it recently and loved it. The very first one, the crappy red Mazda, had turned out to only *look* as if it had had an easy life; alas, it hadn't. Piece by piece, slowly but surely, something under the hood had broken until eventually, five months later, the transmission crashed. It would cost me over a thousand to repair it, so it was more economical to buy a new used car. That one, a Nissan, lasted me a whole year when one day, as I was driving to teach one of my aerobics classes, the oil got so low the engine exploded. Car number three, a Ford Taurus, was great. I had no problems at all with it because I had learned from my mistakes: Before I bought it I had it thoroughly checked out and I also made sure all fluids were always topped off. But as fate would have it, it got totaled in an accident. I sincerely hoped that my current car would be my last for a while, as buying a new car every six months or so was becoming a bit expensive.

Much like Ruth had claimed, it wasn't difficult to find Dr. Webster; her brown wooden house with its black tar roof was clearly visible from the street I was driving on. Due to heavy traffic, it had taken me twice as long as expected to get there, which didn't exactly make me feel more favorably disposed toward Dr. Webster. Me being *very* sweaty by now of course only added insult to injury. At any rate, I parked my Mitsubishi on the side of the road and headed toward her home/office.

When I couldn't find anything that looked like the main entrance, I walked up on the house's wooden veranda that seemed to surround the entire building. I followed it as it turned around the corners. It stopped abruptly before a thin door with a window. This door led into what had to be the kitchen and was slightly open, as if the house wanted to whisper, "Come in". I peeked inside, not quite sure what to do. It was so quiet it didn't appear like anybody was at home. Could this really be the right house?

"Helloo?" I projected loudly into the house, hoping for an answer from somebody.

"Yeees, III'm heeere," a woman's voice answered from somewhere deep within. "Come on in!"

I pushed the door open all the way and entered. Just like I had suspected, there was a kitchen behind it. It smelt of recently chopped onion and raw meat. As I passed the sink, I spotted a white plastic bowl on the area next to it, jam-packed with what might eventually become the meat sauce of a pasta Bolognese. I continued out into another room, a huge room, it turned out. Little light entered into it from between the cracks of the venetian blinds covering the windows, so it was hard for me to see much at first; my eyes needed a few seconds to adjust themselves from having spent the previous hour out in bright sunshine. Then I spotted a large sofa upholstered with drab-colored canvas. It had wooden armrests. The table before the sofa was created in that same type of cherry tree wood. A medium-sized TV hovered before the table. Right as I discovered the many shelves covering the walls filled with rows and rows of different-sized and multi-colored clay pots, a soporific voice to my right spoke.

"You must be Julia."

I spun around and looked in the direction of the voice. In the other end of the long room – far, far in – a woman somewhere in her late forties sat behind a potter's wheel. Apparently, she had been in the midst of shaping a substantial piece of gray clay into something. She wore a pair of big bottle-bottom glasses and her short hair, I noticed, possessed precisely the same color as her sofa. Her eyes lingered on my face (or at least I think they did. It was hard to tell through those thick glasses). There was a slight smile on her lips.

The first thought crashing into my head was that this indeed must be the wrong house because it couldn't be possible that this pottery-making woman could also be Dr. Marit Webster – or could it? Well, she *did* know my name...

"Yes, I'm Julia," I confirmed, still on my guard.

"I'm Marit Webster," the woman said slowly, standing up and wiping off her hands on a towel she conjured up out of nowhere. I saw then that she wore a baggy batik tunic and a pair of ill-fitting washed-out jeans, a choice of attire that made her look more like she had escaped the seventies' anti-war movement or Woodstock or something and somehow traveled into the future rather than just being another part of the sleek minimalist mental health workforce of the late nineties.

"Why don't you have a seat and I'll be right with you. Would you like something to drink?"

"Some water would be nice," I said and took a seat on the dull-looking sofa, wondering what type of psychologists these egg donor agencies worked with. (Dr. Webster was used by the doctors in Glendale, as well as PFA.) Definitely not the type that appealed to me, that was for sure. I liked professional, effective people and this woman with her hippie-style and slow motion speech seemed to be neither. As I waited for her to return, I studied the many different pots fighting for space on the shelves. The sheer amount of them was unsettling to me, because if she was the creator of all those, she couldn't be doing much else but sit in front of that wheel all day long. This, for a busy psychologist, struck me as rather weird. About a minute later she appeared again with a note pad, pen, and a glass of water in her hands. She had a seat on a chair right opposite me, one that was situated before the table. Then she handed me the water and contemplated me silently for what felt like at least thirty seconds.

"So how are you doing today, Julia?" she said all of a sudden.

Her abruptness took me by such surprise I didn't know what to say at first.

"Euuuhm…good."

"That's good."

Silence.

"How do you feel about being an egg donor? How are you coping with it?" The words seemed to be crawling out of her mouth.

"I feel great," I answered curtly.

"How do you feel about another woman carrying your child?"

"I don't feel it's my child really."

"But how can it not be your child?"

"Because it *isn't* really my child."

"I see." She removed her glass-covered eyes from me and scribbled something on the notepad in her lap.

I didn't feel like explaining myself further and I didn't care if that appeared rude; I wasn't the one that had requested this meeting. I didn't need it. I still could not understand why I had to come here and have my emotional stability evaluated just because I chose to supply other women with my eggs for money. I could understand a psychological evaluation – one where they put you through some actual *tests* – might be necessary for a surrogate mother, someone who would carry a child in her stomach for nine months to whom she probably would establish a connection, but not for an egg donor – and especially not since the equivalent wasn't a requirement for *sperm* donors.

I had thought about this a lot lately, as Ruth had kept pushing for me to get my butt over to the psychologist and get my mental health evaluation taken care of. The more I thought about what it was that I was doing – supplying infertile women with the eggs I didn't need – the better I felt about it. How could I not? It was a *win-win* situation for all parties involved! And, to be completely honest, getting paid lots of money to spread my genes around the world was a pretty cool feeling. The fact that so many people wanted to have kids with my genes was a great ego kick.

"So, if it isn't your child, Julia, whose is it?"

"Well, *genetically*, of course, it is my child, but since I don't give birth to it or raise it I don't really consider it 'my' child." Did I have to spell it out for her or what?

"Then whose child is it?"

"It's the recipient's child." Jesus! Why did she keep harping about this whose-child-is-it-business? I wasn't planning to ever kidnap the products of my eggs in the future, if that was what they feared. I had a hard time as it was supporting myself.

I knew now that I definitely did not like this woman. It was hard to put my finger on precisely why, because it wasn't just these last questions that irked me. And, sure, I was sweaty and irritated, but it was more than that. It was all of her, the whole package. I couldn't stand the way she scrutinized me, as if I were a little speck of something she had put on a slice of glass to view under her microscope. The way the words crept out of her mouth, one every ten seconds, certainly annoyed me. I wanted to tell her to remove that patronizing smile that danced over her lips every now and then. It wouldn't surprise me if she felt the same way about me, as I wasn't acting very friendly.

"I understand that you have donated your eggs more than once. Why did you want to become a donor, Julia?"

"Because it's great money!" I spat out. Would I get fired now? But then, the rebel in me submerged. I felt like pushing her buttons some more. "Actually, I kind of like the idea of spreading my genes also. The more people like me in this world, the *better*." Now I was convinced I would get fired. As soon as I got home there would be a message from Ruth wondering why I had to do this to her and myself, why I couldn't just say the right things like everybody else. But I didn't care any longer; it had felt great letting that thought out into the great wide open.

"I see." Again Marit scribbled something on her notepad. Then she looked at me and smiled an obscure smile.

"How do you and Ruth get along?"

Why did she ask that? "We get along great."

She kept asking her weird questions and I kept answering them for about twenty more minutes. Finally she stood up. I followed her example.

"Well, that's it for me, Julia," she said, adding, "Thank you very much for coming."

"OK, thank you," I replied. A brief moment of silence ensued as we stood there face to face. I expected her to say something about how I had done in this evaluation, but she didn't say anything. Not that I blamed her; I wouldn't like to tell somebody the bitter truth to their face either. It was so much easier having somebody else tell me that I wasn't suited to be a donor. Oh, *why* did I have to be one of those stupid people that speak first and think afterwards...? See, by now, I had come to regret my sudden need for mutiny, as I did *not* want to stop being a donor. And considering how much this psychologist, this pop-psychologist because she didn't strike me as a real psychologist – even better, this *pot*-psychologist because clay seemed to be all that she was good at treating – anyway, since she hated me as it was, I was sure she would make me sound ten times worse than I had really been.

I said good-bye and left her house with mixed feelings, part furious, part defeated.

As I drove back to my apartment I hardly even noticed how hot it was despite being stuck in traffic once more; I was much too irritated. And had I noticed it, it would have been good; it would have been the perfect punishment for screwing up my good fortune.

The very second I entered my house I threw myself on the phone to check if there were any messages. There was one – from Peter. With determined fingers, I punched in Ruth's phone number; I figured I might as well hear the bad news immediately.

As soon as Ruth answered I asked her if she had spoken to Marit.

"But weren't you just there?" asked Ruth confused.

"Yeah, like an hour ago. So she hasn't called you yet?"

"No. Did something happen? Something that I should know about?"

I could act rashly, but I wasn't a complete idiot. I wouldn't do the same mistake twice. The truth was I did not know for sure that Marit actually hated me or that I had made such a bad impression on her. Since I hadn't been favorably disposed to her or her doings with me, it could very well be that I had unconsciously looked for reasons confirming the chip on my shoulder. It is possible that if I had met her under completely different circumstances, I might not have been bothered by her slow motion speech or casualness. Maybe I wouldn't even have interpreted those smiles as patronizing. So I said,

"No, not exactly. I was just curious what she had to say about me. It went great."

"Well, that's great, Julia! So I gather it wasn't as bad as you had first thought then?"

"No, that's true. It wasn't *as* bad as I had thought."

"I knew you would like Dr. Webster when you finally got to meet her. I knew y'all would get along just fine."

"Oh, I wouldn't go *that* far," I responded with mischief. Even though I had decided to try viewing the session with more maturity, I wouldn't start lying now all of sudden. "I have no opinion about her."

"Now, I don't believe that, Julia," Ruth laughed. "You *a'lwaaays* have an opinion."

Touche'.

"OK, I'll admit it. She wasn't really my favorite type of people. And I don't like pots."

Ruth let out another hearty laugh.

"You're too funny, Julia!"

▼▼▼

When I spoke with Ruth a couple of days later, I had almost forgotten about the evaluation. I didn't really think I would get fired from my position as super donor with her, so I had soon stopped worrying about it; after all, I probably hadn't behaved quite *that* badly. However, I didn't expect Marit Webster to give me a rave review either. Because, according to Ruth, Marit had found me to be not only very intelligent but also well balanced and sympathetic! I was flabbergasted, so flabbergasted at this outcome I was sure Ruth must be lying to protect my feelings or at least exaggerating Dr. Webster's words. Either that, or Dr. Webster must have been a pot psychologist not only in terms of clay but in terms of *pot*, too...

16

TO REFER OR NOT TO REFER FOR MONEY

For the third time I wandered around my new one-bedroom apartment. It was absolutely gorgeous, spacious and full of light. I couldn't get enough of it even though I had already seen it plenty of times during the four days I had lived there so far. The floors were made of shiny hardwood; the walls in all rooms were painted a stone-washed white, which, in combination with the two arched entrances to the living room reminded me of old stone houses in the Greek archipelago; there were lots of big windows, as well as lots of closet space; and the ceilings were high. Also, not to forget, there was an eat-in kitchen. This was truly the opposite of my previous place, that's for sure!

I took a seat on the top one of the couple of steps that constituted the little stairway connecting the hall with the lowered living room and tried to imagine what this airy room would look like after I had filled it with furniture and finished decorating it. At this point, only the bedroom was fully furnished. The rest was completely empty except for my TV, a bookshelf, and my recently purchased computer that I had placed in the living room. Surely, it would be fabulous. Surely, here I would be happy at last.

See, just like I had switched cars frequently over the years, I had switched apartments more often than what one ought to – three times to be exact. But at the time of each move, I felt I had no other option. The first occasion, as you know, had been because Ilse and I weren't a great match as roommates and also because I wanted to live alone anyway. However, Casa Bonita, as you also know, was anything but a great place to live. Still, as bad as it was living there, I did make myself stay there for more than six months. What pushed me over the edge in the end was the fact that the gang living above me decided to settle their disputes with guns instead of fists for once. I don't think I will ever forget the thunderous sounds waking me up in the middle of the night, sounds that I knew before the police flooding the apartment building moments later informed me had come from a pistol being fired over and over again. The following day I gave my thirty-day notice. My third apartment, a studio, was all right albeit a bit tiny. Here I stayed for a total of two years. Other, more abstract reasons prompted me to move this time: As I had gotten older, I had begun to doubt my sudden change of careers more and more. Did I really want to become an actress and stand-up comic after all? The conviction that had filled me earlier was no longer as strong. Sure, the acting classes I took were a lot of fun. Pretending to be someone else, getting under the skin of a complex character and learning what drove her to make the choices she did in life was exciting. Then, standing on stage, receiving appreciative laughs and earth-shattering applause for the jokes I told was truly intoxicating. Unfortunately, more often than not, as I mostly performed for an audience consisting of other comics, the laughs and applause rarely happened. I quickly came to learn that the occasions were sparse when a struggling new comic got the opportunity to perform before a group of regular people that sat there because they wanted to laugh and enjoy themselves, not because they were eagerly – and often cantankerously – awaiting their turn to occupy the coveted stage. Yet, as much as I enjoyed playing someone else and the few glorious moments of "killing" – comic jargon for giving a great performance before a good audience – I noticed that I found even more satisfaction in simply writing and creating good material in general.

I got plenty of help creating and developing my stand-up act from Peter. He and I had become the best of friends ever since we met that one night at a comedy club. These days, I socialized with him a lot more than with anyone else, mostly because he was the only one I knew who was as deeply focused to make it in his chosen career as I. He was a lot more focused than I, actually. I had always been attracted to people with a passion for what they were doing and Peter sure had this. In the beginning of our friendship I couldn't get enough of it and, as mentioned before, I found it tremendously inspiring. As of lately, though, it had begun to get on my nerves. Like, for example, the way he always nagged on me to keep working on my act or practicing my cold-reading skills. Sure, I realized that he did this because he truly wanted me to become really good at what I was doing, and I appreciated that. What I didn't like was that he insisted on telling me what I should talk about on stage, what he felt I was all about, instead of listening to what I wanted to say. If I came up with a bit that I liked, he always had to change it, adding his personal touch to it. Having a lot more experience and skill as a writer than I, his ideas were often excellent, but it didn't exactly help me developing my own skills as a writer or my true stage persona. And when we were doing readings of plays in his house, he nearly always found something wrong with how I chose to do it, even though he had instructed me to do it the way I saw the character. Then he would play my part his way. Being such a confident and seasoned actor, usually, his interpretation was better, convincing me he was always right. Again his teaching method didn't help me improve as an actor but made me insecure and distrustful of my instincts. In short, I felt he was not only controlling me but suffocating me, too.

At any rate, I thought the multiplying doubts I had begun to experience in the last few months might really be the fruits of my depressing surroundings. If I moved to a bigger, much nicer apartment in a residential area that actually felt like a home instead of continuing to live in a dark tiny bachelor pad located right by a five-lane road, surely they would disappear. And today, as I contemplated my new beautiful apartment that presently bathed in sunlight, I was convinced I was right.

I looked at the clock on my cell phone. Fifteen minutes remained before I was scheduled to have coffee with Elizabeth, a Norwegian model I had befriended at the gym recently that wanted to become an egg donor. I stood up and walked in to the bedroom to get a last look at myself before I left. The image bouncing off the large mirror was that of a recently turned 28-year-old dressed in very washed-out blue tights, an old

T-shirt, and flip-flops. It didn't please me. I was wearing what I had come to dub "The L.A. Uniform" – old pair of tights or shorts, baggy T-shirt, and flip-flops or maybe sneakers. The eternally warm weather seemed to extract variations of this particular outfit from every Angeleno that didn't work in an office with a strict dress code. I wasn't any different. Due to how my life had shaped up, I just about *always* looked like this lately. For example, I no longer went to school at all; while still in class, I had felt a twinge of an obligation to at least try putting together some kind of look other than beach bum. I no longer taught aerobics classes but instead my personal training business had grown and now not only did I train out of a gym but I also went directly to people's houses. It is hard to get away with a pair of cool pants, a great top, and nice heels in these environments. Then, as the L.A. nightlife had steadily lost its magic appeal to me, I had almost stopped going out to clubs and bars, which had been my last resort for dress-up.

I didn't really mind this new super-casual style of mine. It was only once in a while that I longed to wear "real" clothes, things like I had purchased each time Los Angeles's short version of winter came around, a season where temperatures often remained mild, although rain did fall every now and then; nice things I had bought on sale thinking that soon I would find an opportunity when I could use them. And today was one of those times; I felt the irrepressible urge to revolt against the casualness of California (and myself ultimately) and wear something *nice* for my coffee meeting. If I was to be on time, though, I had to act swiftly. I dug into my closet to see what kind of hidden treasures among the many rows and stacks of dull everyday clothes I might find. A few minutes later, I looked like a new person.

Elizabeth was already seated in the Starbucks patio when I arrived. Like expected, she was dressed in the L.A. Uniform – in a white tank top, a pair of cutoffs, and flip-flops, to be more specific. She looked straight at me, so I waved to her. Somewhat awkwardly, she returned my greeting. As I came up before her, I realized why: She didn't recognize me.

"Hi Elizabeth," I said. Her pale, erratically freckled face exploded into a wide smile.

"Oh *hiii*, Julia!" she said. "I hardly recognized you! You look so different in those clothes! You look great though, like such a *business-woman*. Are you going on an audition for something?" (Luckily for me, Elizabeth didn't belong to that group of Norwegians Ilse belonged to, those bent on speaking their mother tongue as soon as they spotted someone from the same part of the world as them.)

Elizabeth was referring to my going-against-the-grain outfit: a pair of black dress pants, a white shirt, a gray form-fitted designer jacket I had bought for about a fifth of its original price, and a pair of stiletto heels. I had felt great in it while observing myself in my bedroom mirror minutes earlier, very stylish yet professional; now, however, as I looked at all the people scattered throughout the sun-drenched patio, I felt more out of place. It seemed as if today, everybody had dressed even *more* casual than normal. Oh well. What had I expected?

"Something like that," I lied in response to her question.

Elizabeth was already sipping on a large latte, so I went up to the counter and ordered only one for myself, as well as a coffee crumb cake – despite a personal promise I had made yesterday to cut down on sweets.

With the items in my hands, I took a seat in the chair opposite her. After a brief exchange of rather meaningless matters taking place at our mutual gym, she asked me to tell her more about what it was like to be an egg donor. I dutifully recited my experiences, making sure I didn't leave anything out. At this point, I had explained the same things so many times I hardly had to use any brainpower; I just opened my mouth and the words began flowing out. And I could tell that to Elizabeth they seemed fresh and spontaneous.

Elizabeth would be the fourteenth or maybe fifteenth girl I referred to Ruth. Referring donors came easily to me, as I seemed to meet a new person every other day, had an outgoing personality, and a firm belief that becoming an egg donor was a great thing to become if you could. Women trusted me – and so did Ruth. She thought that I had good judg-ment. To her, I was the perfect spokesperson. She knew women's faith in me was key not only when it came to selling them on the idea of becoming donors (which pretty much everybody I spoke to became unless they had some kind of physical restriction) but also when it came to the occasional girl who worried excessively regarding whether or not to donate her eggs. Ruth would give her my number so that I could calm her down. Usually, after a phone conversation with me, her veteran donor, where I candidly told the girl about how easy I found it being an egg donor, the deal was closed.

It didn't take long for Elizabeth to make up her mind. She definitely wanted to become a donor; like all of us, she could use the money. She had recently turned thirty-three and the modeling gigs weren't as steady or as lucrative any longer. The one problem with Elizabeth was her age; for the most part, women above thirty weren't accepted. I thought that she still might have a chance, though, since, except for her age, she possessed every other desirable quality: She was tall and slender with face and hair like that blond bombshell Hollywood actress Heather Graham. She also struck me as bright. So I decided that I would talk to Ruth about her after all. Maybe Ruth would make an exception when she saw Elizabeth. I had a feeling she would; Elizabeth just looked so youthful and healthy, like she could produce many fertile eggs.

We continued to discuss egg donation when I noticed that my latte must have traveled through my inner tubing faster than an ice cube in hundred-degree weather would turn into water. I needed to take care of my bladder immediately, so I excused myself.

As I sat there, inside the neatly kept public bathroom of Starbucks, an idea emerged within me. I wasn't sure whether the cozy but definitely corporate coffee shop environment that had surrounded me for the last half hour could have spawned its sudden birth, or whether the fact that I today was dressed in a business-like manner could have something to do with it. It didn't matter. I thought the idea was brilliant and wondered how come I hadn't thought of it before.

So I had understood from the beginning that the common term for a woman giving her eggs for money was "egg *donor*" even though, in reality, we were nothing less than sellers of eggs. It had taken me more time, however, to grasp that what Ruth did was pretty much the same as that what any other type of broker or agent did. For each girl she matched with a couple, she got a commission. I wasn't sure exactly how large it was or how it worked; all I knew was that, without me, she would have made about fourteen times less of whatever this amount was since that was the number of girls I had referred to her throughout our seven-donation long relationship. The ubiquitous entrepreneur in me was making itself noticed: If Ruth could make a living selling women's eggs to other infertile women, why couldn't I... I had already been doing this work for as long as we had known each other – for free. I didn't think it was more than fair if Ruth started giving me some kind of finder's fee from now on. I thought 100 dollars per person would be a good amount. With my own experiences as a multiple donor, gregarious personality, and ease to win over women when I wanted to it could be a golden opportunity for me. I should, like Ruth, put my talents and efforts into a more organized system.

The more I thought about this, the clearer my vision became. Considering the apparent never-ceasing demand for donors, there was a lot of money to be made here. Maybe I could figure out a way to approach a bigger number of women and suggest to them the possibility of becoming a donor. If they were up to it (I knew plenty of low-income women would be up to it), we would all benefit from it: the girl herself, the receiving woman, Ruth, and I. What was wrong with that? Nothing I could think of. As I washed my hands in the cold metallic sink, I smiled to myself in the mirror, feeling almost spiritual. Maybe the business of egg donors in all its shapes and forms was my destiny in life...

"What's that smile all about?" Elizabeth asked as I returned a minute later, the same smile apparently decorating my face still, and took a seat in the white chair. By now, I was feeling like a bona fide businesswoman. And I no longer felt out of place.

"Oh, nothing. I just had a great revelation," I replied.

"Oh, yeah? Like what?"

"Like how I should not have another one of those coffee crumb cakes, even though they are delicious and I want one more badly. They have a tendency to make me fat."

"Right."

Some things are better left unsaid.

The next morning I sat on the floor next to my cordless phone, about to make the call to Ruth, this call that would take our mostly amicable professional relations into a different realm.

I wasn't completely convinced she would *love* my proposal because about six months earlier, during one of our many phone conversations, I had insinuated that I was making her a whole lot of money due to my referrals. I could tell that she wasn't exactly pleased that I had brought it up, but then one day about a week after, an envelope containing a check for a hundred dollars and a note thanking me for my help signed *Ruth* arrived in my mailbox. Neither of us ever brought up the issue again.

I had been thinking about my revelation all day long yesterday, and all night long, too. I had plotted and schemed ways of how to approach different women. All the money I would make! Why *didn't* I think about this before? I mean, it was just *such* a great idea!

Yet, more or less from the moment I stepped inside my apartment yesterday after my coffee date with Elizabeth, a tiny doubt had clung to me like a wet T-shirt, along with a mild discomfort that had begun to tickle my stomach. I couldn't place my finger on what this was. Wasn't it just a marvelous idea becoming Ruth's subagent? Pure logic told me that yes, it definitely was. But something else, a voice forming within me demanding its proper attention, said something else.

Then, throughout the night, I dreamed vividly. I often did, so it wasn't exactly out of the ordinary. I could only remember bits and pieces of this private variety show such as the following scene: I was sitting in a beautiful house somewhere high up, perhaps along Mulholland Drive, sharing a bottle of wine with some friends. Ruth and Dr. Goldberg were there, as well as the balding doctor I found so hot. He and I were married. We were talking and laughing, contemplating Los Angeles by night, the many rows and rows of glittering lights in every conceivable variation of yellow and orange and pink. All of us were wearing expensive jewelry and elegant designer wear. The phone rang. I walked over to answer it. It was Ilse.

"I just found out that Isabella hung herself in her apartment. She's dead…"

"What! What are you saying…?" Isabella was one of the over 100 donors I had referred in the past year. "It can't be true! She's the second one in just a month…"

The phone slipped out of my grip. I ran out of the house onto the street and threw myself toward the many rows and rows of glittering lights. The feeling of the imagined fall expressed itself so sharply in my stomach I was subsequently tossed out of la-la land, back into the real world.

This particular part of my dream had stayed with me all morning, at least the essence of it. It was impossible to get it out of my head.

I decided I would go clean the stove because of the abundance of food stains I had decorated it with yesterday while cooking dinner before I would make the call to Ruth; it had to be done at some point and now was as good a time as any. In fact, now was a *great* time…

As I stood there scrubbing the enameled surfaces free of Ralph's Supermarket's own brand of pre-mixed marinara sauce, I began to understand where the continuous discomfort stemmed from, why I was seemingly involuntarily questioning my decision, and – most of all! – how come I was all of a sudden filled with such desire to make my stove appear brand-new before I called up Ruth: What if I referred somebody who deep inside *didn't want to* become a donor? Somebody who couldn't handle it? Not that I really believed that some girl would commit suicide just because she donated her eggs and then regretted it – that was just some crazy dream – but still. I knew that if I would be making my living on other women donating their eggs the money might start to influence me, start to rule me in a way I didn't like. I knew I would feel weird knowing that, when I spoke to a girl about becoming a donor, depending on her decision I would stand to either win or lose a hundred bucks. I would feel terribly biased. Treacherous. Even though I did believe egg donation was safe, and I wanted to believe that every woman was perfectly capable of determining if she can or cannot handle becoming a donor (without first being evaluated by a psychologist), I knew this was just wishful thinking. Because not every woman saw life the same way as I did. What if just *one* of the women I had referred, who had seemed to know exactly what she wanted, who had seemed fully mentally stable, five years down the road inexplicably changed her mind? What if she would start to regret what she had done? What if she would never get over it? Or, even worse: What if her biggest dream was to have kids and she – due to extreme misfortune – would become infertile from the procedure? It wasn't likely, but it *could* happen. I didn't think I would like to live knowing that I, in extension, would be responsible for this.

No, becoming some kind of professional egg broker seemed just too weird for me. In the end, since I wouldn't be able to do it, I never seriously brought up my proposal to Ruth. But at least something good came out of this: My stove had never looked better.

17

AN EXPANDING MIND

I looked down at my naked thigh, trying to find an area of skin that hadn't been bruised. It proved quite hard. I was getting genuinely tired of looking like I was a heroin addict each time I went through the donation process. How come I could never ever learn how to perform this simple task correctly, this chore I had performed on so many occasions by now? When I was at the clinic and a nurse stabbed me with the tiny needle, no swollen discolorations ever resulted. If they had figured it out, how hard could it really be? Apparently, for someone like me, *unattainably* hard.

Again, here is the proper manner in which to inject oneself, as it had been explained to me *repeatedly* by at least three different sweet and patient nurses: First you must wipe the area of the bottle through which the needle is supposed to penetrate with a serviette dipped in alcohol. This step is very important if you want to diminish the risk of catching bacteria that can infect the stick, something that is quite common. Now you stick the needle through the area, but make sure the plunger is pressed all the way in first. Then you turn the little bottle upside down so that the liquid is easily accessible. As you begin to pull the plunger out of its confinement, you will notice how the syringe is slowly but surely filling up. (You might also spot some air bubbles, but forget about these for the time being.) When you reach the desired marking on the tube, you need to stop pulling. Now it is time for the actual injection. But wait! *Don't forget to first wipe the area that will be injected with a serviette dipped in alcohol! Very important if you want to diminish the risk of...* As you subsequently bury the needle into your flesh having first flicked away any air that could be trapped in the liquid, don't go crazy and start pushing it into your body. First – and listen carefully now, take notes or whatever you have to do, because here is where the trick comes in, this for me unachievable ploy – you only want to push the plunger halfway in, or until it hits the surface of the liquid. *Then* you want to pull the plunger back *up* again. If there is no blood suddenly mixing with what is already inside the syringe, you are good to go. Go ahead and push that plunger all the way down and feel the slight chill when its content enters your body. No bruises will or can form now because you haven't hit a blood vessel. Sounds great, right? Well, I'm living proof that this is not a full-proof method, because for some reason – despite having taken extra pains to follow it step by step during my last three donations – I almost always managed to hit one.

I was now about to do my ninth donation, though, technically, it was my tenth since my previous one – the "real" ninth – had been terminated in the fourth week. They paid me 1,000 dollars for the trouble.

I had gotten so used to just sailing through my procedures without any kind of complications that Ruth's phone call had seemed unreal to me at first: She just *had to* be pulling my leg when she told me the recipient's body wasn't responding properly and therefore the cycle was likely to be canceled. Of course, the doctors had tried their best to make the donation work one way or another still; for example, they kept me on the Lupron a week longer than normal, resulting in me having to take estrogen pills to make up for the every day decreasing level of estrogen my body suffered. As Ruth handed me the pills, she let me know I might experience slight discomfort before the pills went to work: severe fatigue, edginess, headaches, becoming extremely sensitive emotionally, feeling down, insomnia. When she discovered the confused look on my face, she added, You know, things like you usually experience when you have PMS. I nodded as though I understood perfectly, even though I had yet to be subjected to this feminine sickness.

Luckily for me, out of her itemized ailments related to estrogen depletion, only fatigue, some headache, and slight edginess during a couple of days came my way. But they soon disappeared.

The terminated donation was a bit of a blow to my financial situation. Not having any reason to believe this particular cycle was to end prematurely, I had already spent almost half of the 5,500 dollars – my current fee – by tying it up in one of my different projects. This fall the project had been financing two one-act plays Peter and I were putting up in which we were both starring. Peter had written them especially for us. In our fervent pursuits to be signed by good agents, the two of us were always trying to come up with new and/or original approaches to woe these elusive creatures and this was our latest and most elaborate one. We had spent months to prepare and rehearse these plays. From morning to night we were busy with something in connection with it, as every single detail just *had* to be perfect! See, I couldn't bear struggling for much longer. I needed to make it soon! After having pursued acting for close to three years and stand-up comedy for two, it was fair to say that I was getting a bit stressed now. Sure, I had done a few minor things during this time. Through the manager I had worked with briefly, I had gone on some major auditions in which a couple of them the casting directors had even called me back. Yet, I felt as if I was getting nowhere.

So I had to come up with 2,500 dollars just two weeks after the donation was supposed to have been completed to cover the financing of the plays. Thanks to an experiment I had agreed to undergo simultaneously with the ninth donation, I still made the payment. In this experiment I was part of a test group of donors so that a certain aspect of the cycle could be studied in depth. It ended the day before the termination and I received 1,500 dollars for it.

Unfortunate as it was for everyone involved having to end the cycle, it did serve as a reality check for me: A month later, when Ruth called to offer me a tenth donation, I had begun to wonder whether or not I might be overdoing this donation-thing. I mean, after all, we were talking *nine* cycles already. Perhaps I was putting my health in unnecessary danger. Could it really be safe to go through yet another one?

"Oh, honey, it's perfectly fiiine!" Ruth emphasized from her end of the phone line. "You're fine, *just fiiine*. I know a woman who donated *sixteen* times in the eighties and she's doing great. No problems at all. She has kids of her own now, too."

"Yeah, I guess you're right. Maybe nine aren't all that much. And I do feel great," I said, pleased with Ruth's unexpected response. I had been sure she would say that yes, maybe it is time to stop now. Thank God I was wrong! I really didn't want to quit quite yet.

"No, it really isn't. If you ask me, I don't think you have anything to worry about at all, even if you decided to do *five* more. But of course, it's up to you if you want to do them or not. Ultimately you will have to decide that. It's your body."

That was so right. It was my body and I was the one and only person deciding what to do with it. Throughout our years together Ruth had made a point of showing how much she knew what this small but important right meant to me. I had always been grateful to her for that – even when she forced me to go to the psychologist. I knew she wasn't the one who had created the policy; she was just the messenger. I understood there were certain guidelines she had to make sure all her donors followed. And at least she had *tried* getting me off of it. She claimed she had let all the doctors know I was the most emotionally stable person she had ever met and therefore there was really no need for me to go. But they hadn't wanted to take any risks.

Based on Ruth's passionate advice and my own wish to continue, I decided I would donate a few more times – maybe not *five,* but definitely one or two more times. However, I wondered if I was making the most out of myself and my eggs. Lately, I was reading stories that popped up with increasing frequency in the news about how some egg donors made truckloads of money, and I was seeing with my own eyes how ads looking for donors in the Backstage West and the L.A. Weekly offered more and more money. With my track record and the seemingly never-ceasing demand for my eggs and therefore my genes, I could be making a lot *more* than the 5,500 dollars I made these days, couldn't I...?

The steady, rather steep incline over the years of the compensation donors received indicated that other women must think the way I did.

From my readings, I learned the following: In 1984, when egg donation became available to the public, donors only got paid 250 dollars. By 1987, the price had risen to 500 and it reached 1,500 in 1993. In the middle of the nineties donors were compensated 2,500, a sum that doubled to around 5,000 by the end of the decade, in other words, now.

More than ever, it was clear to me now that money talks; obviously, *no* women did it for free. It felt good knowing that my gut feelings had been right from the beginning.

Nonetheless, I still went ahead and began my ninth (tenth) donation with Ruth. I needed some more time to figure out what my next move should be – if I really wanted to take my business elsewhere, if it was worth it. See, there was no getting away from the fact that it was quite comfortable to just wait for Ruth to call and tell me when and where my next cycle would take place. (I was patronizing a variety of hospitals these days.) I wasn't sure if I was willing to give that up.

If I wanted to make more money, I had two options: I could either continue working with an agency – an agency that would offer me more money – or I could go private. By private I meant answering some of the many ads people like the Jamesons placed in the papers and online. There were just so many of them! For the most part, they were modest ads that offered a bit more than the market price; say, between 5,000 to 10,000 dollars. Then we had the ones where the parents were smart like Einstein, looked like super models that could moonlight as basketball players, and were extremely healthy – or they just wanted a kid with such attributes. These people were willing to pay outrageous sums for the right donor, usually around 50,000 dollars. Then there were a few willing to pay up to 100,000 dollars (!). The only downside to this was that the prospective parents often seemed to be blond and blue-eyed – or, again, simply wanted a donor with those characteristics. I wasn't sure whether they would be interested in somebody with light green eyes and dark blond hair like myself.

As my ninth donation came to an end in February of 2000, I read about a couple from San Francisco willing to pay exactly that amount –

100,000 dollars – for the donor of their choice. Oh, my God, I thought upon having read it; here we had the *perfect* ad: They were looking for a healthy donor under 30 (I), at least 5'8" (I), dark blond (I) that was a proven college-level athlete. That last requirement I wasn't sure if I could prove, as, even though I definitely was athletic, I had never competed in any sports on college-level. I thought I should still apply though. I hoped that, when they met me, they would like me so much they wouldn't mind this minor flaw. It was worth a try.

However, while the possibility of making 100,000 dollars from just one donation was incredibly tempting, I have to admit that I did find it not just eccentric but rather freaky actually that somebody was willing to pay that much money for a kid when they could have one for ten or even twenty times less. I knew from seeing with my own eyes that there was a bunch of very smart, pretty, athletic donors around in that price range. Then again, as I was pondering this couple (and others, too, that I had read about) who was I to judge them and their values, their way of viewing life? Assuming they were indeed themselves carriers of the genes they requested from their donor, did it really follow they were also whacked out just because they were willing to pay lots and lots of money for them? I didn't think so. They might just be very rich and generous people, people that truly appreciated what their donor did for them; I, if anybody, knew that it was a lot of work and responsibility involved being a donor. The more I thought about this, the more I realized it applied even if they *didn't* carry these super genes. As a matter of fact, it had nothing to with whether they did or not. If you had the money, why *not* pay to get a child with the absolute best genes, much better than the ones you yourself could supply it with? We all know that a healthy, smart, and – even more important – beautiful child would have an easier time in life. This is even a *scientifically* proven fact. A beautiful child is usually more popular, won't have a problem finding a partner, and will get hired faster. Humanity is – whether we like it or not – obsessed with good looks. We all want what's best for our children, don't we? In other words, weren't these elitist requirements simply an act of love? And, didn't this mean that somebody willing to pay such an extreme amount of money would also love and cherish this child incredibly?

Yet, even though I wanted to believe people only acted with sincere, good-hearted goals in mind, I couldn't shrug off the increasingly stickier notion that it was something rather sick about the whole situation. There was a flipside to this brightly shining coin of pure intentions, a side that was dark, dirtied with the idea that your child *had* to be the best, the brightest and most beautiful. What if *this* was the end goal of these people? Unfortunately, considering the competitiveness of today's society, it wasn't at all an unlikely thought. Just imagine, in that case, if the kid would not turn out to be born with these great genes? Parents with good genes aren't a guarantee the offspring will possess the same genes; it just means there is a much higher probability. What if the donor egg of these elitist parents resulted in an overweight, short, and not very smart kid? Could these parents still find it in them to love it? If it turned out these parents were a couple of weirdos, I would have a hard time living with that knowledge.

Still, I didn't know which foot to stand on, because, after all, this second, scarier assumption was just that – an assumption. How was I to know?

Thinking this over some more, I decided I would go ahead and apply. Then, if they picked me, I felt confident enough I would be able to tell from speaking with them for a few hours whether they were psycho or not. If they were, I could always back out.

Fortunately, I was never placed in this position (and also *un*fortunately since it meant I would miss out on the chance of making 100,000 dollars…). I never even got through the initial screening process, as the woman I spoke to over the phone told me that if I couldn't prove I was a college-level athlete, they wouldn't consider me.

That was the only private ad I actively pursued. When it didn't work out, I kind of lost my drive to keep pushing it. It seemed to be more trouble than it was worth and, in the end, I don't think I would have liked being a private egg donor. The agencies might pay less, but in the long run they were safer and you knew you were dealing with established professionals.

I did call a couple of other agencies, however. When I found out they all paid roughly the same amount as Ruth or just slightly more, I figured I might as well stay with Ruth till the end; 5,500 bucks was not *that* bad... And with her, at least I knew I was in good hands; if something happened to me, Ruth would help me out.

By now, almost four years from the day we first met, she and I had become even closer. The more we got to know each other, the more we realized how similar we were. We were both strong, independent women that couldn't handle insincerity. We knew exactly what we wanted out of life and weren't afraid of saying so. And we were both also women not originally from America. Ruth was of Irish decent. She had moved from Kork to Charleston, South Carolina with her mother and father as a six-year-old. Even though she evolved to what most would consider a typical Southern Belle, complete with the hospitality and drawl and all, she still never forgot her roots. Every year she and her husband, who she had met in Charleston, and son and daughter spent a few weeks on the green island, visiting relatives and enjoying the Irish way of life.

Though I knew she took a lot of pride in her Irish ancestry and everything that had come with it, there was one thing that bothered her, one matter she was deeply torn about – her strict Catholic upbringing. At the one hand, as a moderate Republican, she believed in tradition and religion, especially when it came to bringing up her own kids; she wanted to bring them up according to her and her husband's Catholic religion. But she was also aware of how being Catholic had screwed up her own life. During more than a few phone conversations and a couple of dinners, she told me about how she felt severely repressed sexually, how she loved her husband but didn't want to have sex with him. Knowing me and my Swedish liberal view on sexual matters, she even asked me for advice.

Such were some of the things we discussed. She also came to see both my plays. I felt certain Ruth and I would stay friends long after I was done with being an egg donor. Never could I imagine that she, deep inside, was not a strong person at all.

Not at all.

18

A Suicidal Mind

When I woke up early in the morning two days ago, I didn't feel great. Not as if I were about to come down with the flu or anything, just a bit strange; edgy, kind of sad. A light headache lingered toward the back of my skull. Staying in bed and sleeping for the rest of the day, or at least a few more hours, seemed like an awesome idea, but as I had two personal training clients that morning, one at seven-thirty a.m. and one at nine a.m., this wasn't feasible. Basically, I felt generally unhappy, the way one sometimes does for no special reason at all. Of course, usually when I felt down like that, there was a very specific reason for it, namely, lack of sleep. I had been pretty sure that must have been it this time as well since the night before I had stayed up late and watched a movie, resulting in me only getting six hours of sleep. Six hours might not be a disaster for most people; for me it was. I'm hypersensitive to not receiving the right amount of sleep. To function perfectly, I *had to* get eight hours. Nine times out of ten when I slept insufficiently, I developed a different personality. I became moody and miserable. People that knew me found it almost scary how I turned into an entirely opposite person, like Dr. Jekyll when he became Mr. Hyde. What made this situation even more irritating was that there was nothing I could do to make it go away. I'm not the type of person who, when they haven't slept enough, could take a nap during the day to make up for it. No, I just had to bite the bullet and wait until it was evening again. The good news was that the following morning, I was back to normal.

So I did find it a bit odd when the next day, I was *still* feeling weird – even more weird than previously actually, very depressed. And I could have sworn that the night before I had slept enough. Oh well. I guessed that I hadn't and that was why I felt like crap once more. Though, by now, it was definitely beginning to get on my nerves; a third day of this self-imposed depression and I would go completely nuts. To make sure it wouldn't happen again, I took a sleeping pill when I was about to go to bed that evening. It had the desired effect; I slept like a baby for nine and a half hours straight. The following morning I was convinced my moodiness had finally been taken care of because, as I sat up in my bed and yawned big, stretching my arms up into the air, purchasing a gun to blow my head off no longer seemed like a viable option.

This neutral frame of mind lasted as I went about my morning business. I turned on the radio in the living room, enabling the local morning-DJ and his team to do their thing for me on my favorite station. Then I went out into the kitchen to make myself a sandwich and heat up some water for my tea. I opened the fridge and removed two pieces of pre-sliced wheat bread from the freezer, which I placed in the toaster. I filled the teakettle with water and put it on the stove. It wasn't until almost ten minutes later when I had poured the boiling water into my pink mug that contained an Earl Grey tea bag and the contents of three packs of Equal, the toasted bread had become a cheese and ham sandwich, and I had positioned myself with those items next to the radio, that that same strange sense of darkness and uncomfortable negativity crept over me anew. But even as I noticed it growing bigger, slowly filling my insides, I hoped that, if I ignored it, it would just go away. See, this time I knew it had nothing at all to do with me not sleeping well. It wasn't due to physiological reasons.

So it had to be psychological.

Evidently, I must be turning into a self-pitying grouch, I concluded. I refused to let that happen. I took a bite of the sandwich and concentrated on how to chew it properly, not just gulp it down like I normally did. I had a sip of the steaming tea, thinking about how much I loved tea that was this hot. I listened intently to the radio show, to what the DJ and his sidekick were currently discussing. But despite being the big fan that I am, I couldn't stomach listening to it this morning; everything they said annoyed me. So I switched off the radio. I went back into the kitchen to double-check that there was fresh food in the bowl for the cats I had recently picked up at a shelter, and that their water had been changed. I couldn't seem to remember whether it had been done this morning or not, even though it couldn't have happened many minutes ago.

As I came back into the silent living room, I picked up my sandwich and tea mug from where I had left it next to the radio and brought it with me to the off-white sofa I had bought at IKEA a year earlier. I placed the items on the coffee table and took a seat. For a few seconds, as I sat there contemplating my breakfast, I was sure that I felt better again, that I had actually managed to make this unsettling mood disappear.

But then, as I reached for my barely begun sandwich and my tea, I noticed something was bothering me. Really bothering me. What was it *now*? I wondered irritated. Could it be the silence this time? Normally, I always listened to the same radio show in the mornings as I ate breakfast; it had become a sort of ritual for me. It could be the silence, but I wasn't sure; I just knew I felt weird, bad weird. And this time the weirdness didn't creep over me like it had five minutes ago. No, it was *attacking* me... As suddenly and completely as if somebody had thrown a sheet on me colored with that particular emotion, an intense despair lowered itself over me. Something inside me told me to stay put in the sofa, something that made me incredibly heavy, so I remained seated, staring before me. My eyes filled up with water and soon tears were outlining my cheeks.

What the hell was happening to me? Why was I so sad? It didn't make any sense. I didn't have anything to cry over, at least not more than usual. As a matter of fact, the more I thought about it, the more I realized I had fewer reasons than ever. The last couple of months I had been happier than I could remember having been for a long time. My blissful state stemmed from my decision to give up trying to become a famous actress and comedian. Being on stage wasn't really for me, and I had come to understand this at last.

The realization had hit me like a stone in the head, as I met for the second time with a rather important agent who dealt only with soap operas. He had called me in from one of my mass mailings of headshots. He liked my look and the two scenes I performed for him. The way he saw it, we faced only one problem to get me hired easily – my accent. If I wanted to work with him, I had to get rid of it completely. So the next day I bought a couple of tapes and began practicing every day on how to speak American English. Four weeks later, I thought I had gotten the hang of it, so we scheduled a new meeting and I did two new scenes. No, the accent was still there, he claimed. As he carefully explained I had to keep working on it, I suddenly wondered what the heck I was doing there listening to how vital it was for an actor to be able to handle any accent in the world. It wasn't that it didn't make sense what he was saying. I totally agreed. The part that didn't fit the equation was that I didn't care whether *I*, Julia Derek from Sweden, could ever handle any accent in the world. It simply struck me as such a frivolous goal to pursue. It was in that instant I knew acting was not what I should be doing with myself – and especially not if I had to work so hard to get hired.

It wasn't quite as easy to give up the stand-up comedy. I very much enjoyed the rawness of it, the immediate gratification you got from performing live, successfully or not, and the many interesting, wonderful people I met while pursuing it. The problem with pursuing it, however, was that 90 percent of the time was spent trying to find decent stage time. And that was a huge problem. If you didn't get to work on your act before a decent audience a few times every week, you would never get any better. In the end it just wasn't worth all the time and effort for me. I didn't need to be on stage and receive all that attention *that* much any longer. (When I started out, I had thought I wouldn't be able to live without it.)

But I knew I wanted to keep doing something creative, artistic even. So I decided I should get back to the very reason why I had first come to America, namely journalism and writing, particularly writing. Coming to this conclusion had served as a catharsis for me. It ejected all the stress and confusion my life had been filled with the last year. My identity crisis had finally come to an end. For the first time in many years I felt centered, calm and relaxed. A new chapter of my life was about to start.

So my moodiness definitely didn't seem to be contingent on any external factors taking place in my life. And it couldn't be that I had finally developed PMS because I wasn't exactly about to have my period. I was in the midst of doing my tenth donation (which was really my eleventh). I doubted these unexpected depressed emotions had anything to do with it since I had never before felt even remotely down during any of my donations. As a matter of fact, it was even *more* unlikely this time: They had put me on birth control pills to calm my ovaries, as these had been acting up a bit lately. The estrogen in the birth control pills was supposed to regulate my hormones so that I wouldn't feel bad in any way.

I forced myself to think about the day before me, hoping that this would put me in a happier state of mind – or, at any rate, a tearless one. Thank God I didn't have any clients until five p.m. on Thursdays! I had to go buy cat litter, take the car in for an oil change, buy some groceries, and then I had planned to write on a novel I had recently begun. "OK, Julia, let's go," I said out loud, trying my hardest to cheer myself; I might as well get started immediately so there would be more time left over for me to write. Wiping my face dry with the back of my hands, I made myself stand up. But as I had only moved two steps forward, a new batch of negative thoughts overwhelmed me, even stronger than before: Oh, why bother doing any of it! Wasn't it all just meaningless? The last thing I felt like doing was to go and change the oil of my car. What difference did it make if this car, too, would explode, like that other one? And it certainly didn't make any difference if I had extra time to write. Who did I think I was anyway? Like I could write a novel – in English, on top of it! It was laughable actually that I had gone around for two entire months believing that I could write an entire novel in English. I suddenly found myself seriously wishing I were dead. It would be so much easier. What did I have to live for anyway? I hated my life, people didn't like me, I couldn't stand my job as a personal trainer, the guy I had a crush on at the gym had a girlfriend – and I had at the age of *almost twenty-nine* decided to change careers again, in other words, a move bound to fail. That was just obvious. And then I was fat and ugly, on top of it. Everything sucked. I walked inside my bedroom and threw myself on my unmade queen-sized bed. The tears flooded my eyes once more as I hid my face deep down in the pillow. I could feel Inga and Fabio, my two adorable kittens, jump up on the bed and restlessly pace around their owner. They could sense my misery and it was evident it bothered them. Fabio, the black one, tried squeezing his snout in between the mattress and me. Then, unexpectedly, feelings of anger began to mingle with the sadness. Oh, stop it, Julia! I screamed into the pillow, as if that would make me snap out of this inexplicable mood. It's not all that bad! Stop acting like a five-year-old! I turned around and slapped my face a couple of times. But it didn't help – if anything, it seemed to make my tears fall faster. Apparently, this sense of impending doom, this monstrous feeling that had me stuck in a snug embrace, wouldn't be shaken off that easily. Since I couldn't find any more power within me to fight it, I gave in and let the tears have their course.

The sheer intensity of these emotions must have made me fall asleep because when I lifted my head from the wet pillow and looked over at the alarm clock next to my bed, the big red numbers said, ten a.m. I hadn't slept for long though, only twenty minutes.

As I let my head fall back onto the pillow, I noticed that – as suddenly as it had appeared – the violent need to cry had vanished, as if all that it had wanted was for me to sleep a few more minutes. Alas, I couldn't claim my mood had become cheerful and positive as well; no, I could still sense the gloomy darkness looming there inside me. It had just decided to retreat for a moment, to go smoke a cigarette or something. And the last thing I felt like doing was to get my butt in gear and get on with things. But I couldn't waste one more day. I couldn't just lie on my couch watching TV and stuff myself full with chocolate like I had done the past two days. I *had* to pull myself together. With an immense amount of willpower, I made myself stand up. Maybe if I took a shower this strange mood would disappear at last. Maybe it was something that could be washed away like dirt.

As I stood there five minutes later, letting the warm soothing water follow every curve of my body, I did experience relief. Thank God, I thought; so I must have been just tired. It is all going away now. And this time the uproar did stay away for quite a while.

My trip to Petco and the supermarket went without any glitches. The oil got changed, and every other fluid that needed it, was topped off. An hour later I had returned home. As I sat there before my computer, about to start writing, I realized there was no way I could today and, considering the weird mood I had been in lately, I decided it probably wasn't a good idea to push it. So I just went ahead and cleaned the apartment. It could do with a thorough cleaning anyway.

It wasn't until hours after that I began to feel bad again. I was sitting waiting for my client to arrive in the little private training gym half a block away from my apartment building where I nowadays trained many clients. A powerful edginess seemed to enter each one of the millions of pores in my skin. Anita – my client – like so many other times, was late. Normally, it didn't bother me much, but right now, even though she had called to let me know when she would be there and I didn't have other clients afterwards, it was pissing me off. *Really* pissing me off. One of the other trainers, a sweet guy who very much resembled Tom Cruise and was also waiting for one of his clients, attempted to have a civilized conversation with me; something about how he thought I should stretch both before and after I ran on the treadmill and not just after like I usually did. I could hurt myself badly, he claimed. I knew this wasn't really true, but I also knew what he was trying to say and, in a way, he had a point. Unfortunately, as I was feeling at the moment, rapidly deteriorating inside, I couldn't handle talking to anybody, so I excused myself and went out to the balcony. My sudden departure must have come off a bit weird, but there was nothing I could do about it.

As I stood there looking out at the traffic that moved along narrow Melrose Avenue, contemplating all the tiny unsuccessful stores filled with cheap flashy clothes only tourists, transvestites, and strippers perhaps would buy, seeing how dirty everything was, how it all seemed to be covered in ugly, depressing graffiti, I began to cry. But not the small, controllable tears of this morning that one just wiped away and the cry was pretty much over. No, these were of the type where it feels as though somebody has turned the personal faucet within you not one but various turns, and it is just gushing. What was going on with me? *Why was I crying like this?* I had been standing out here on this balcony a hundred times, staring at the exact same things, and never felt anything even remotely sad about it. Because even though it wasn't the most glorious sight in the world, neither was it particularly depressing. I took deep breaths trying to force myself to stop crying. It didn't appear to be helping much. I turned around slightly to see if anybody behind me inside the gym could see what was happening to me, if Tom Cruise's twin brother was trying to figure out why I had just left him like that in the middle of our conversation. But he was no longer within view. The rest of the people were busy either doing lunges while holding onto dumbells or push-ups on their knees while their trainers kept a watchful eye over them. And there was still no sight of Anita. Now I was just thankful she wasn't here yet. I sincerely hoped that by the time she came I had found a means to control myself. I turned around, my tearful eyes pointlessly scanning the streets again. That was when I spotted Anita appearing from behind the corner, moving rapidly toward the door leading up to the gym on the second floor.

▼▼▼

I don't know how I did it, but somehow I found it within me to stop crying just before Anita stepped inside. I guess my body had that same reaction a mother has when she sees her child stuck under a car and finds within her an extreme, previously unknown strength to lift the car. I just couldn't survive if I began to alienate my clients, both for economical reasons and out of pride. I explained the swollen redness of my eyes that was so evident by claiming my contacts must have broken. Then, training Anita proved to be therapeutic for my wretchedness; or, at any rate, it took my mind off of it.

Happy I had managed to get through the training session without any major incidents, I walked the few yards back to my apartment. For the rest of the night I would just take it really easy, like reading one of the books I had borrowed from the library the other week; do anything more strenuous and, surely, my feelings would go haywire again. I could just pray the end to my strange mood had arrived at last.

So I sat down on my sofa with an apple and *The World According to Garp* by John Irving, one of my favorite books. I had already gotten through half of it.

Usually, I loved Irving's writing style, finding it very easy to read; however, this evening, the words just seem to be floating before my eyes, making incoherent statements. I read the same sentence over and over. And, meanwhile, Fabio was having fun with my sweater.

"Stop it, damn cat!" I screamed, roughly pushing him away, as he for the third time tried to climb my back. He looked at me, his owner, uncomprehendingly, with his huge green kitten eyes and let out one of his signature wailing meows. It wasn't like me to be so harsh when he misbehaved. I stared back at him. For the first time since I got him, he angered me. And it was an anger that rapidly escalated.

"You damn stupid cat!" I yelled, hoping that he would go away. But he didn't budge, just kept looking at me. I thought that, if I ignored him, my anger would soon dissipate and he would eventually stop appointing me the tree or the hill or whatever I was to him in his game. I gave my attention back to Garp and his adventures.

But I wasn't able to make the sentences into a flowing narrative. Why was it so damn *impossible* for me to concentrate? This was just great: Now that I no longer felt like crying, I was developing *other* problems! Then, from the corner of my eye, I saw that Fabio approached me anew, like a hunter on the sly. Before he could jump on top of me, I caught him. Holding his little black body firmly with both hands, I looked him deep in the eyes. He let out another loud meow. The sound prompted the seething anger I already felt with him to amplify ten times. An urge to throw him into the wall in front of me started to grow within me, but before it got so big it would take me over completely I realized what I was doing. I let the cat down on the floor and just sat there taking shallow breaths. The violent urge disappeared and I felt numb instead, entirely void of emotion, a blank slate. What the *fuck* had I been thinking? I was suddenly scared of myself. How could this little cat have instigated such an extreme rage within me? He wasn't behaving any differently from other days. He and Inga always clowned around like that, behaving like two maniacs, running from one side of my spacious one-bedroom apartment to the other, climbing the curtains, the sofa, the plants, everything that was in sight. And I usually loved it when they went on a rampage! So why was this minor misbehavior from Fabio upsetting me this much then? It took a lot more to set me off, normally. What was going *on* with me?

Reading might not be such a great idea after all, so I put the book away and switched on the TV. Rachel and Monica of the ever so popular sitcom *Friends* were having a discussion over some guy Rachel had gone out with. As Monica took a bite of a chocolate chip cookie, I noticed that I was hungry. I looked at the clock on my cell phone. It was seven-ten p.m. When did I eat the last time? It didn't take me long to realize it hadn't been since breakfast, when I had that sandwich, which I hardly had even begun. So, basically, I hadn't been eating anything since the day before! For something like that to happen to me, to forget to eat, never occurred. It just wasn't something I had an issue with. I sometimes *wished* I forgot, since I'm cursed with a close to insatiable appetite (though, to balance that out, I'm blessed with a high metabolism). Still, today it had happened.

I went out into the kitchen and opened the fridge to see what I could make myself for dinner. There wasn't very much to choose from, only a couple of yogurts, butter, ketchup, a bag of pre-cut lettuce, and some onions and tomatoes. So it looked like it would have to be tuna and tomato salad this evening. I was pretty sure one can of chunky light tuna was somewhere to be found in the cupboard.

It was when I turned around to open one of the cabinets and retrieve a bowl to put the lettuce in that my eyes caught the knife.

I stopped moving and just stared at it, as it lay there by the white stove, this long gleaming bread knife with its black plastic handle I used for everything. I suddenly found myself wondering how it would feel if I used it on myself for once, if I cut a little here and a little there. I reached for it and my fingers wrapped themselves around the black handle. Terrible despair and loneliness enveloped me in that moment. My eyes filled with tears, tears that competed amongst each other to be the first one to hit the kitchen rug. It would be just as well if I took care of it now; I couldn't stand living another day of this miserable, meaningless life I was leading anyway. My whole existence was a fucking joke. It had always been a joke, from the day I was born. I was such a mistake, such a failure in everything. And the reason I felt like I did now must be my subconscious's reaction to my decision to give up pursuing stardom, the only chance I had to finally make something of myself. I hadn't really wanted to give all of that up.

But if I hadn't, why had it made me so damn unhappy in the end?

As it was, the thought of getting back into that world of phoniness, of crazy, lying, self-absorbed people, and vicious backstabbing only served to accelerate the ever-growing urge I had to cut my wrists. Then, as though two big hands of steel cupped my skull and squeezed it like a walnut, a screaming ache entered my head. It hit me with such fierceness that the urge to end everything moved into the background. All I could think of instead was how to make the pain stop. I threw the knife in the sink and sank down on the floor, gripping my head from the forehead. Oh, my God, was all I could think, *what's happening to me?*

I'm not sure when I understood what was going on finally. The only thing I remember was that at some point I punched in the number to the nurse on duty at the clinic and that I broke down as soon as she answered.

"I can't keep taking those damn pills," I cried uncontrollably into the phone. "They're driving me *crazy*. I'm even having thoughts about killing myself...."

"Julia," she said sharply, "take a deep breath! You're not going to do anything so stupid! And you won't have to take any more pills. If you don't take any more you will soon be feeling good again. When was the last time you took one?"

"Last night…"

"Don't take any more pills, Julia. Do you hear what I'm telling you? Don't take any more!"

"OK…"

"And don't you even think about something so stupid as killing yourself, Julia! You just feel like that because of the hormones. These birth control pills are not the right ones for you. Do you hear what I'm saying?"

"Yes," I mumbled. Her harsh manner had the desired effect. I was sobering up; the headache even seemed to be retreating.

We spoke for a while more, until she was fully convinced that I was no longer at risk of making real of my first hysteric threat and that I was aware these horrible feelings would go away as soon as tomorrow probably. Apparently, it wasn't unusual that women had bad reactions to birth control pills.

I felt much better as we said good-bye at last and I hung up the phone. The tears had dried up. I didn't feel like using that bread knife on myself any more. The headache was still there, but it was more of a controllable, dull pain now, not that raging, maniacal one from fifteen minutes ago. Just the mere act of having had this talk with the nurse had been enough for my pain to settle down. Hearing somebody give me a plausible reason as to *why* I was suddenly living this hell had been a crucial part in the challenge of harnessing it.

I stood up and stumbled into my bedroom. Moments later I had fallen asleep on my bed, still dressed in my trainer's outfit.

19

PRELUDE TO DISASTER

"**S**o how are you doin' now?" Ruth wondered, as we spoke over the phone in the early evening the following day. She had just found out about the ordeal I had gone through the last few days. "It must have been so aawwwful for you! You really should have called me."

"I didn't feel like being a whiner again. I have already whined enough to you," I said. I was referring to an intimate conversation we had shared over dinner a couple of months earlier, a conversation of which certain parts still embarrassed me. It had taken place right before the inevitable falling out between Peter and I. I would never forget how patiently Ruth had been listening to me that night, as I was going on and on about how terrible my life was. I told her about all the problems I was having as of lately, how I had no idea what I was doing with myself and how I felt like I must be an extremely confused person, a person who had no grip on anything. In the end of my long searing monologue I had even cried a little, something I had never done in front of Ruth prior, and this was the one part I *especially* wished I had managed not to do. Well, I tried consoling myself, as this moment of weakness haunted me every now and then in the days afterwards; when all was said and done, I knew that I should not be worrying about having lost face. After all, it was *Ruth* I had been speaking to, a mature woman and good friend who had always understood me, not some shallow starlet I had befriended while attending a party. Also, now, in hindsight, it had become clear to me that my complaints had been fairly trivial really, along the lines of what most people experience as they slowly but inevitably head toward the big 30 – they had just felt severe to me at the time, as I was in the midst of them. In exchange, instead of dessert with the coffee, Ruth had treated me with some more of her own predicaments with sexual repression and how that related to the happiness of her marriage.

"Oh, don't you ever say that, Julia! You didn't whine, you just told me about how you felt about certain things taking place in your life in that moment. I'm sure I whined much more than you did about my marriage. But anyway, you're feelin' better now, right?"

"Yes, *much* better, it's almost like night and day. It's weird. I almost don't even remember how I felt. I just know that it was awful."

When I had woken up in the morning, I soon noticed that I was continuing on the same note as I had gone to bed on – away from depression and violent, suicidal thoughts. I still felt a bit weird, but not even remotely similar to the day before. It was obvious now that the nurse and I had been correct: My body simply couldn't handle the birth control pills I had been on to calm my ovaries.

So I don't remember in which exact instant it had dawned on me that I had had a very brief but identical reaction to birth control pills in my early twenties, but when it did I had thrown myself on the phone and called up the clinic; I just knew I had to get off these pills – or I would do something really bad. The enormous relief I continued to experience at having finally figured out the root to the evil overtaking me with such slow confidence was difficult to describe.

"So do you think it's OK if I continue the donation without taking birth control pills?" I asked Ruth. "Can my ovaries handle it?"

"Well, the doctor said it should be OK. And personally, speaking from my own experience with other donors, I'm sure everything will be fine. You don't have anything to worry about."

"OK, that sounds good," I said, preparing to hang up and get on with the evening; I had a lot to catch up on after these past three fruitless days. "But I think this will be my last donation though. I'm pretty sure that this was my body's way of telling me it's just about had it. Don't you think?"

"I'm not so sure about that, Julia. You haven't gone through *that* many donations. It's more likely that you had – like you said yourself –

a really bad reaction to the birth control pills. We gave you the wrong type, the ones with lots and lots of progesterone. You probably wouldn't have had *any* problems with the ones that have a much higher level of estrogen. You're just extremely sensitive to this particular brand, which isn't unusual at all. But, of course, if you don't feel like doing any more donations, that's fine. Although, don't make that decision based on what happened these last few days because that wouldn't be fair. If we keep you away from these pills, you'll be fine. *Just fiiine.*"

"Yeah, I guess you're right. It was just the pills. So maybe I'll do one more after this one. But I'll have to think about it first."

"That's right, Julia. You think about it."

I hung up the phone and went over to my sofa where I sat down. Before I got started with tonight's writing of my novel, which I had already titled *The Sammie Club*, I wanted to relax a few minutes. I wanted to savor the feeling of being in complete control of my mind again, to thoroughly experience how it was not to be depressed. You only know how wonderful and important, how *indispensable* that neutral state is, if you have once been so severely depressed, despaired so much, you seriously felt there was no reason for you to keep living. Because only now, at seven p.m., did I feel as if I was back to normal again. The only residue seemed to be a certain feebleness in my limbs and a very light headache. But it didn't matter; in no way did these minor remains affect my mind. The optimism that was so characteristic of my being had returned in full. Everything would be all right one way or another.

▼▼▼

About ten days later it was time for me to get started on the heavier drugs, the egg-producing, big-needled ones. I couldn't wait to get this donation over with because even though my mood remained on top as soon as my body had gotten rid of the last trace of the progesterone-overloaded birth control pills, something didn't feel quite like it should; something I couldn't put my finger on. It was just a sense I had, that followed me everywhere like a shadow. It was as though something tried to tell me it wouldn't work out this time. In short, I was feeling slightly weird but not exactly depressed.

So I wasn't very surprised when the doctor who I had worked with during my last two donations – Dr. Williams – told me after my second ultrasound that my eggs didn't seem to be multiplying like they should. Not to worry though, he added. We won't give up yet. Keep taking the drugs; it might just be a slow start to this cycle.

On the fourth ultrasound, things hadn't progressed much, however, and I felt increasingly strange. A headache chased the sunlight that woke me up in the mornings.

I couldn't concentrate on writing my novel. The few follicles I had developed weren't as healthy and big as the doctor had gotten used to from me. My insides looked like a washed-out memory of previous cycles. Dr. Williams still told me to go ahead and draw blood downstairs since whether we would do the retrieval or not in the end depended on my estrogen levels.

I went down to the bottom floor of the clinic where the laboratory was located and blood tests were taken. That stunningly beautiful black woman was working today. Looking at her always made me think of Cleopatra with a myriad of small braids. Out of the three people working down there, she was my favorite. In comparison to the other two, she always seemed to be in a good mood and chitchatted with me about this and that. She was also the only one aware of me having quite a few donations under my belt. I had happened to disclose this well kept secret to her when I first met her – two and a half donations earlier – as she carefully explained to me what she was about to do before injecting the needle. I know, I know, I had told her. And then I had added in a low voice: Promise me you won't tell anyone, but I'm actually not new at this. I've donated *eight* times before! I was very proud of this track record of mine. Oh my! she had replied, looking as impressed as I had hoped.

She sat on a chair reading a magazine when I entered, giving me the impression that she had nothing else to do but wait for me to come along. I went up and took a seat on the stool on the opposite side of the table.

"Hi, Julia," she said, looking up from the colorful pages and smiled. "Drawing some blood today, are we?"

"Yes," I said, trying to sound cheerier than I felt, because by now I could feel how the darkness expanded around me by the minute.

We sat in silence as she got to work. I gave her my arm like I had done on so many other occasions, the one with the easiest-to-tap vein, and she proceeded to wipe the area that would be penetrated. She handed me one of her clay-like rubber balls to squeeze until my vein was the most visible. Like always, as she was about to stick me with the thick needle, I tried but failed to look away and then, even before the needle entered, I squirmed like an upset three-year-old trapped in a baby carriage. I watched as the vial attached to the other end of the thin plastic tubing filled with that dark, dark red liquid that was my blood.

"So which number is this cycle?" she asked, abruptly cutting through the entrancing silence.

"It depends on how you count them," I replied, probably coming off more mysterious than what I had intended.

"What's that supposed to mean?"

"If you count the terminated one I did in November."

"So, if you count that one, which one would this be?"

"The eleventh."

"That's a lot."

"What do you mean?"

"That's a whole lot of cycles."

I didn't answer. I just watched her as she wrote my name and phone number on a sticker that she put on the vial filled with my curiously dark-colored blood. As she placed it in a stand with other vials, she looked at me.

"Are you sure that's good for you to be doing that many donations? I've never heard of anybody doing that many."

"Well, so far I haven't really had any problems," I lied.

"I see," was all she said. I got ready to leave. I thanked her and said good-bye.

"Thanks yourself, Julia. You take care of yourself now."

That would be the last time I saw her.

◥◥◥

The minute I got home I ran into my bedroom and threw myself on my bed. I felt like crap again and it was clear to me why: My hormones were not the way they were supposed to be. My estrogen level must be plummeting again.

Even though it wasn't really necessary for me to get it confirmed that this cycle would be canceled, I still lay there, waiting to hear it out in the open; sometime this evening I would be told about it over the phone. The depressed state made me heavy, tired, unable to move. I tried sleeping away the growing discomfort but without success.

I don't know for how long I remained there staring at nothing before the sharp signal tore through the thick silence of my apartment. At this point the heaviness had turned into a severe sadness, creating an abundance of tears that streamed down my cheeks in a steady, ever-building manner. As I answered the phone, I did my best to control myself:

"Hello..."

"Julia, it's Rosa from the doctor's office."

As opposed to all the other nurses I had worked with, nurse Rosa and I had never gotten along. She reminded me of that uptight, unhappy egg donor coordinator at the Maryland Fertility Group from four years earlier. Each time our paths crossed at the hospital there was a powerful tension in the air, making it uncomfortable to breathe. We often ended up arguing, mostly because of her tendency to explain in detail everything I was supposed to do and not do while going through a cycle: when to take the drugs, how much of each drug I was supposed to take, how not to pour the powder into the saline solution but the other way around, when to go and draw blood, not to forget to call the clinic when my period arrived, when to schedule for ultrasounds, etc., etc. She insisted on going through this twenty-minute speech each time it was her turn to hand me a box of fertility drugs, even though having worked with me since my third donation at the West Los Angeles hospital (she had been transferred to this particular hospital these days) she knew perfectly well that, by now, the only thing that I *wasn't* an expert in when it came to being a donor was how to avoid bruising myself while shooting up. Not once had I made a mistake or misunderstood any instructions given to me.

I had always had a hard time with people talking to me like I was an idiot, and that tended to happen quite often nowadays due to my accent and therefore immigrant status. (The fact that I had begun to highlight my hair, something that certainly made me look very Swedish, didn't precisely improve that situation.) But, knowing this, I knew also that I had developed an almost paranoid vigilance against being talked to condescendingly, which had pushed me to first give people the benefit of the doubt; on about half of the occasions it turned out it was my own mind playing games with me.

I had long ago concluded that Rosa didn't belong to the mind-fucks department, though. With her I knew it was personal, that she didn't really like me. I still don't know exactly why that was; and when I asked Ruth about it the other day, she only explained it by saying that Rosa was having personal problems and that I shouldn't worry about it so much; it didn't matter. Also, she had added, we should be grateful Rosa wasn't aware of just how many donations I had done. (Rosa thought this would be my sixth.) If she did, we would really have something to worry about.

I had to admit that despite pretending like I couldn't care less, deep inside it always kept bothering me, in much the same way Dr. Goldberg's look of indignation had bothered me each time she saw me the last year at PFA.

At any rate, it struck me as uncannily appropriate that Rosa was the one delivering the crushing news to me this evening, continuing on the pattern of misery she had seemed bent on establishing in my life prior.

"We're going to have to terminate the donation. Your estrogen levels are not where we'd like them," she said curtly, managing to sound even colder than she usually did when she spoke to me.

"...huuh...?" This was all I could get out when I spoke at last. I had meant for it to come out a loud and powerful WHAT??!!, clearly conveying the dismay I experienced at the sound of her words. It surprised me how it upset my already upset state so much more, having merely *heard* her say them, even though I had known all along. But it was the final blow to whatever there was inside me that kept up a tiny, indefatigable fight not to give in to the depression about to fully overpower me.

"But you can't do that..." I tried screaming, but instead it traveled over the phone line as a meek, beseeching whisper. "You have to take the eggs out of me... I can't stand feeling like this. I can't take any more of it." I hadn't forgotten how, during my sixth donation, the doctor I had been working with had explained that it didn't make any sense for a donor ready to lay her eggs to keep them in her body; it would just make her feel even worse. The fear going through me at the thought of feeling even worse than I did right in that second was impossible to put into words. I just knew I had to get those damn eggs out of my body or I would go completely nuts.

"You can't just leave me like this... You have to give me something to make me feel better!"

"Julia, get a hold of yourself!" Rosa said sharply. "I'm sorry to hear that you're feeling so bad, but there is really nothing that can be done about it than to wait it out. It's not dangerous. Your body is just depleted of estrogen at the moment. As soon as the levels go up, you'll feel better again. It shouldn't take more than a week."

I couldn't believe my ears: a *week*!

"A *week*? Are you kidding?"

"No, Julia, I'm not kidding." Rosa's voice assumed an even icier tone, as though I had gravely insulted her. "There's nothing that can be done. You just have to wait it out. Do you understand?" It wasn't a question precisely.

"What about those estrogen pills? Can't you give me some estrogen pills? Wouldn't that make me feel better?" I was getting desperate now.

"I don't think it would really make a difference. Besides, we don't have any here and the pharmacy is closed."

"But I can go to the pharmacy here where I live. Like I did last time."

"All the doctors have left for the evening, so nobody can write you a prescription for it. And I really have to go myself, Julia." It was clear to me that she had no interest whatsoever in making me feel better. I gave up.

"OK…"

"Call us on Monday, if you're getting worse. Then we might be able to get you some pills."

"OK," I replied, finally beaten down. It wasn't until we hung up that I realized it was only Friday today: I had the weekend to look forward to before I could even begin thinking about getting any help.

▼▼▼▼

"But I felt different, though, than when I was low on estrogen that first time, you know, that time last November," I explained to Ruth, as we, two weeks after that distressing phone call from Rosa and one week after I had bounced back entirely, were discussing whether it was safe for me to donate again without my hormones going haywire. We had gone back and forth for a while now trying our best to determine just how likely it was that they would remain stable like they had done during every one of my other donations.

"But Julia, that must be because you took those birth control pills, those, together with your estrogen going so low. That's why you felt like this, there just isn't any other option. Really, it's not at all strange that your hormones were going *crazy*. And the reason your eggs didn't develop like they should this time was because of that new brand of hormones Dr. Williams insisted on using. It doesn't work with you. So it wasn't your fault in any way. I'm sure though, that if you take a rest over the summer you'll be fine to donate once more. Because, you see, I have this great couple that wants you as their donor. They *only* want you, Julia. And the best part is –" Ruth lowered her voice " – they will pay you 7,000 dollars!"

"Wow! That *is* a lot of money! Well, let me think about it for a while, a couple of months or something, and then I'll give you a definite answer, because I'm not *totally* sure I want to do one more. I have to see how I feel. If I have any more problems like this…"

"You think about it, Julia. This couple is willing to wait until you feel you're ready, so that's not a problem. We have a deal?"

"Deal!"

20

ANOTHER VISIT IN HELL

My fifth summer in Los Angeles passed rapidly. I spent the beginning of it in Sweden, my first trip back there in three years. I had what I thought was a serious relationship with a neurotic investigative journalist who I had met in the spring; unfortunately, it would turn out that I was the only one in the relationship thinking so. His name was Joe. Joe's life fell apart when he and his friend failed to become the Woodward and Bernstein of the new millennium. In preparation for the Bush-Gore presidential election, these two die-hard liberals traveled all over the country in search of evidence to support their firm belief that George Bush Jr. was a monster and Al Gore an angel that could do no harm. According to Joe and his buddy, Bush had fathered some kid out of wedlock about thirty years ago. They were convinced that if they could prove this, Gore and the Democrats would easily win the tight race, a race that became even tighter as the actual election was over. And maybe he would have had they managed to find any evidence.

At any rate, since my boyfriend spent most of his time digging for hidden records that must have grown so yellow they would be hard to read by now, I spent a lot of my time hanging out with group of people I had befriended back in D.C. They had, one after the other, also moved to Los Angeles. I enjoyed a final resurgence of my time as a dedicated night-fly; though, now, instead of going to sports bars and glitzy, mainstream clubs we went to edgier places, places I hadn't known existed in this town previously. Once we even ended up at a strip club.

It was sometime during this summer I began to understand that Los Angeles wasn't meant for someone like me. (I think I had known this subconsciously for quite a while, actually.) Instead, I pictured myself more and more living in New York City. I even went there for a brief visit before going to Sweden, my second time in that city. The rawness and crowded feeling I experienced while there appealed to me, as well as the idea of once more living through four seasons each year. I also thought that there it would be easier to meet people interested in things other than working out, the movie industry, and/or how to become famous. I noticed that I missed that special pulse and fast pace you only find in large cities with a heart, something you certainly didn't find in Los Angeles. And I missed how nobody looked at you with lifted eyebrows from inside a car just because you felt like using the sidewalks to walk somewhere. Most of all, though, I discovered how I appreciated the edginess so characteristic of New Yorkers, the harshness, the directness, the mind-your-own-business-attitude that some people consider rude, that toughness one develops when one has to struggle with real life and real problems, and how under the rough surface they proved themselves to be the nicest people.

In September, after having conferred with Ruth some more, I decided that it was time for one more donation, the final one. We both figured that, by now, my body must have gotten enough rest, since I hadn't experienced any kind of problems with my hormones during the summer.

The new doctor I was going to work with – Dr. Dadjaran – belonged to a clinic in West Hollywood, only about five minutes by car from where I lived. Ruth was very excited about him. She had gone through changes this summer as well; for one, she officially went into business for herself and Dr. Dadjaran was one of the doctors she would be using. She went on and on about how attractive, nice, and *eligible* he was. Ruth was well aware of the fact that I was more or less single – my romance with Joe had begun to go sour – and she loved playing matchmaker. I know this was all done with good intentions, but it still irked me slightly, especially when I realized that this doctor was not only unprofessional but also terribly patronizing and pompous. I couldn't understand how on earth she could think that a person like him and *I* would make such a great couple. And even if I had found him attractive, going out on a date with somebody who knew my private parts so much better than my actual face just struck me as too weird. I don't think I would have been able to relax knowing that.

It didn't take many Lupron injections before it became clear to me that this donation would not belong in the same category as the ones taking place during the height of my egg donor days. It would be more along the lines of my very last. Every other day an explosive headache or an extreme crying jag overwhelmed me. I was tired. Worst of all, however, I felt how my self-confidence evaporated and how negativity filled its void. I became deeply depressed. But there wasn't a pattern to this mood. It didn't seem determined to go in any particular direction, like it had the last couple of times, when each day my depression had grown worse. All in all, or at least until I was at the end of the Lupron injections, I felt more good than bad. When I mentioned how I was feeling to Ruth and Dr. Dread – I mean, Dr. *Dadjaran* – they both explained that I had probably become hypersensitive to even mild fluctuations with my estrogen levels. But it didn't really make any sense for me to be taking estrogen pills since, as soon as I would start the stimulating drugs – which would be two days later – my hormones should be stabilizing and I would feel much better again. And, *if* my mood swings were only due to low estrogen, something that wasn't entirely clear, it would take a couple of days before the pills would have any effect anyway.

What they said made perfect sense, so I figured I might as well bite the bullet to the bitter end; as long as I knew there was an end to these hellish feelings that attacked me with increasing frequency, I could deal with them somewhat OK. It would just be a few more days.

When I had been on the supposedly stabilizing egg-producing drugs for about five days and my mood swings only got worse, I began to get a bit worried. How come I wasn't feeling any better?

"Well, the only thing I can think of is that your body really *has* had it now," Ruth offered. "Because, as both you and I know, it's not typical for you to be this sensitive. But then again, one never knows either. Every donation will be different. It's like pregnancies. It's really a shame, though, and I'm so sorry you're feeling so bad, Julia. I really wish that there were something I could do to make you feel better. But you know what?"

"What?" I managed to get out, already knowing what she was about to say. She would give me the same answer she had consoled me with when I had asked her two hours earlier if she had finally found an antidote to my ever-deteriorating mental state. Since then I had been lying on my bed, crying for no reason at all. In the midst of this, Joe had called, asking me to come see a movie with him, but I hadn't dared leave the house, as I knew I would keep breaking apart, making a fool of both him and me. Not being able to do anything about my situation eventually made me so frustrated that I had called up Ruth again.

"On Thursday, when the eggs are out of you, you'll be back to normal again. You'll see, Julia. Just four more days. This too shall pass."

▼▼▼

When Wednesday evening rolled around, only hours before these torturous eggs would be removed from me, I had become so depressed I was literally shaking. I felt more fragile than a doll of the most delicate porcelain, that if even the slightest trauma came my way, I would fall apart and die. When Joe came to pick me up to drive me to the motel where we would be staying the night before – the procedure would take place two hours away from West Hollywood – I had a hard time speaking. Still, in the midst of all of this, I was not fully beaten down, because I knew that, very shortly, I would be a normal person with normal feelings again. In just six hours. An end was in sight.

But then, when the retrieval was over and Joe and I were on our way home in my car, he in the driver's seat and me next to him, I started to cry again. Like never before.

This time, though, it didn't scare me much, as I figured it must be a reaction to all the stress that I had been going through as of lately. It was the aftermath cry, tears of relief. It was to be expected. The tears fell in such fierce strides and for so long you would think I would get thirsty after a while (although drinking something didn't really occur to me). Joe, so used to this state of mine recently, having just about run out of words to say to make me feel better, capped that moment with the perfect comment, "You must really miss your eggs, Julia." Yeah, that must be it, I grinned in between my tears.

As we reached my apartment building he put me in bed and stayed with me until he had to go to work. This was nice considering that we had broken up a while ago and it must have been a pain in the butt to stay with such a blubbering monster like myself. Really, he had already done enough for me by taking the day off yesterday and driving me back and forth. Unfortunately, it didn't matter whether I was alone or not; I still felt like shit. I was sure, though, that after a good night's sleep I would be feeling better again like that time when I got the birth control pills out of my system. By tomorrow I would be fine.

It wasn't until the next day in the afternoon that I was beginning to get slightly concerned because, instead of getting better now, I seemed to get *worse*.

By the hour.

I called up Ruth. She wasn't there, so I left a message. I called up my friends and tormented them some more with my whining. (Thank God I have such great and patient friends!) Late in the evening, when there was no longer anybody left to talk to, I lay on my couch and stared at a colorful sitcom on TV. I have no idea what the hell it was about; all I knew was that resting my eyes on the motions soothed my raging headache somewhat and got me to momentarily think about something else other than how horrible my life was. That was when Ruth finally called.

I could tell from the tone in her voice that she was more worried than she wanted to admit. I even found myself consoling *her* at times during our conversation: I'm sure I'll be fine by tomorrow; it's just taking a little longer for me to bounce back this time; yeah, I'll call you if it gets worse.

Alas, when I woke up in the morning the next day such heavy despair had descended upon me I couldn't make myself get out of bed. Oh, my God, *this just can't be happening,* was all that went through my mind as I lay there, staring out at nothing, wondering which method of suicide was the least painful and most effective. Tears began falling. This afternoon I would have my first client since after the donation. Of course, as I felt in this moment, it would be absolutely impossible for me to train somebody. I would have to cancel our appointment.

Oh well, I thought, surprised at how rationally I could think at the height of the emotional war taking place within me; at least by now it was obvious my estrogen or my hormones or whatever the fuck was going on was completely out of whack. It was also obvious that it didn't seem as though it was planning to regulate by itself. Who knows when it will go away this time? No, Ruth and the clinic would have to help me get to a doctor to take care of this. They have to take tests to determine exactly what the hell is happening and then they have to give me some estrogen or some kind of hormone therapy to make it better. Yes, that was what I would do; I would call Ruth and tell her that. That was the only way.

It was curious, as I lay there trembling with despair, how these thoughts provided me with immense comfort without making me feel physically better. I just felt that, having come to this conclusion, having a solution as to how I would get out of this ridiculous emotional paralysis, I could deal with just about any hellish feeling fate felt like throwing at me. It was OK. And it felt even better when my phone rang and I heard how my six p.m. client cancelled her session for today on my answering machine, which meant that I wouldn't have to cancel on her myself.

I'm not sure how much longer I lay there before I dragged myself over to the phone and dialed Ruth's number for what must have been the three thousandth time since I first found her name in Backstage West. She answered on the second ring.

"Ruth, I need to see one of the doctors," I said, my voice weak. "They have to give me something or take some tests or something. Because something isn't right in my body. Something is missing. I can feel it. I need to get some estrogen or something."

Ruth was quiet on her side of the phone line. I could hear her breathing.

"Ruth... Are you there?"

It took a couple of seconds before she finally responded.

"I'm really sorry to hear that you're still feeling this bad, Julia. Truly, I am. But, at this point, I think it's time for you to find a good therapist. Because this is not normal what's going on here with you. It's clear to me now that it can't have anything to do with the egg donation."

At first I was sure she was joking, to cheer me up maybe, in some bizarre kind of way.

"You really need to get on some anti-depressants. I don't think I ever understood the severity of your depression before."

"Yeah, whatever you and the doctors think is the best. I don't care what you get me as long as I can get out of this terrible mood."

"Julia, the doctors and I can't get you anything. You have to do it on your own."

"There is no way I can do it on my own! Besides, why should I do it on my own? *They* are the experts in this field! They can just take a couple of blood tests and they'll know in a second what I'll need. Then they can prescribe me whatever I should be taking."

"No, Julia." Ruth's voice became stern, as though she had had it with my demands. "Even though I really feel for you right now, I cannot do anything about your personal problems. Do you understand? It's not part of my responsibilities. The reason you're feeling this way has to do with *you*, not the drugs or any hormones running crazy in your body. You yourself were the one telling me that you were having problems lately. Remember our last dinner? It's *you*. You have to get help somewhere."

She paused. When I didn't answer, she continued.

"Promise me you'll get help somewhere, Julia. Get help soon, because it's clear this is not healthy for you; apparently, you have *real* problems. Oh, I wish I had more time to help you, but I have so much on my plate. I'm sure you understand, you know, with my family and my new business and all. I really don't have time. Please promise me though that you'll get help somewhere soon."

What was she *saying*? Was she *really* saying... Yes, she was. She was actually trying to make me think that I was crazy all on my own – that what was happening to me was created by me and me alone. The gravity of her words, of her action, hit me so hard I felt like throwing up. I got so nauseated I don't think I ever said goodbye when we hung up.

It has been going on for many days now, weeks even, this I-don't-know-what-to-call-it-exactly. Depression doesn't seem to be the right word because it is so much more than that. All I know is that it is completely incapacitating. When I think about it, I understand that it has actually been going on for more than a month. It has been going on for so long that I almost believe the notion that this is just part of who I am nowadays.

Some times are not quite as bad as others of course, though those times take place rarely. Those times I can speak in coherent sentences, the crying jags take a break, the pounding headache doesn't block my thoughts and I can almost concentrate so much that I can watch a few minutes of MTV or the E Channel. Light and fluffy, colorful and mean-ingless is the only thing I can stand on TV. Anything else, not just TV but anything that forces me to use my brain even to a minimum, might trigger either another attack of tears or remind my head that it is not perform-ing its new job any longer, that something inside there is supposed to torture me fiercely and continuously.

I learned this lesson thoroughly during one of the first times when I erroneously thought I had become normal again. I felt so great I was convinced it just had to be over entirely, or if not that, at least the tide was finally turning. One sign, as I saw it, was that I had tired of staring at floating pictures of stylized nothing. I needed to watch some movies or something. So, against my better judgment, I ventured out to my car, which was parked just outside the apartment building. I was determined to drive over to Blockbuster and rent a few videos. I got into my car where I managed to get the engine started. I realized then that it would require a rather big effort on my part getting the Mitsubishi out of its crammed-in position, where it was parked between an old rusty Ford Wrangler and a green-gleaming black Porsche.

I made a fruitless attempt at wriggling it out from this stranglehold. And that was all that was needed for another nuclear war to be declared against my head; a headache, overwhelmingly painful, commenced. As if on cue, my tears ducts reopened and began unloading its seemingly never-ending supply of tears. Despair crept inside my spirit through each and every little opening my body possessed, stronger than before even.

This sudden attack paralyzed me for a while and I just sat there inside my car, in front of the steering wheel, staring into the wide blue butt of the Ford. There was no way I would be driving over to Blockbuster feeling like this. Who was I trying to kid? Apparently, I wasn't supposed to go anywhere ever again. I couldn't even get my car out from between two cars that had been parked so close one wondered if they had wanted to make some sort of statement, a statement saying that the three of us had a special connection, that it was important for us to be this close together.

I don't know for how long I sat there before I finally gathered enough strength to get my body out from the light-gray car seat and on to the street, open the door to my apartment that – thank God – was the first apartment on the bottom floor and back inside it. Like a severely intox-icated person I stumbled through the short hallway, down the two stairs leading into the living room, and fell apart on top of that couch I had bought a while ago for money I had made on – guess what? My eggs. I never thought life could be this ironic.

I lay there, waiting and waiting, hoping that this was just a slight relapse, that I really was on my way back to how life used to be before all this inexplicable horror started invading me and turning me into something entirely different, much in the same way a vampire transforms its victim day by day, bit by bit, slowly but surely sucking out all of its victim's life. But nothing changed. My head pounded away, the tears kept falling, and I began to ponder like I had done so often lately whether swallowing all of the thirty-something over-the-counter sleeping pills sitting next to my bed wouldn't be better after all. Sometime, somewhere during this attack I experienced, strangely enough, a renewed desire to watch a video. I suddenly became convinced that if I watched this past fall's season of Sex *and* The City *I would feel much better. I had to see it. Now. So I grabbed the phone and punched in a familiar number. Lately, I have been dialing that number often, so often I don't know why I haven't programmed it into my speed dial already. Actually, I* do *know why; of course I do. I hope that, before it is too late and this person has had enough, I will stop being such a pain in the ass, I will stop calling every half hour, I will hang up after ten minutes like normal people, not two hours when the person I'm speaking to a long time ago has stopped listening but still can't make himself hang up on me. I refuse to turn into this nutcase nobody can stand, not even my closest friends. Putting this number into speed dial would mean that I no longer care, which would mean that my barely-there battle against this alien that is devouring every sane part of me, this fight which I know is going on within me in some tiny, tiny cell, has stopped. It will never stop.*

Jake, the best friend a person could ever have, answered. Like always he listened patiently to my tears and my whining, to my silence as well as to my rambling, to every unintelligible sentence. He agreed to come over after work, which was right now, and take me to Blockbuster to get me my tapes.

True to his promise, he stood outside my door and rang the bell only minutes later. By now, I had managed to pull myself together somewhat. I was no longer a crying, trembling mess. I opened the door, feeling embarrassed for myself and my crazy behavior, praying that I would stay somewhat sane for at least the time it would take us to get to and from the video store.

We drove off in Jake's many-times-recycled BMW. A short while later we were standing inside Blockbuster, passing by rows and rows of videotapes. He told me about something that happened at the gym where he works and I laughed out loud. For a few seconds I had almost succeeded to forget that I was really a bawling, deeply miserable person. I saw the shelf containing the Sex and The City *tapes. Tapes featuring all four characters were there: Carrie, Miranda, Charlotte, and Samantha. I went up to one of the Carrie-adorned paper boxes and removed the box from its place. No videotape was behind it. I removed an Amanda-faced box. There was nothing there either. I removed the rest of the boxes. All the tapes were rented. This reality, which to a normal person would have been merely a bit disappointing, to me, apparently, was the end of the world. I began to cry uncontrollably. Jake was soon standing behind me, his face wearing – against both his will and knowledge, I'm sure – a horrified expression.*

"What happened? What's wrong?"

But I couldn't speak. Even if I could, it wouldn't matter. I couldn't possibly explain why I was feeling so strongly about the fact that there were no Sex and The City *tapes available that night. I just did. In the midst of my tantrum, I snatched a couple of other videos from the shelves that we rented for me.*

Then, swiftly, Jake escorted me out of the store, doing his best to not only shield my face but his face, too, from curious onlookers.

We were sitting in his BMW again, driving back to my house. In the backseat lay the two movies I had chosen, movies I really shouldn't be seeing. One was Girl, Interrupted *and the other was* Crazy in Alabama *with Melanie Griffith. In case you didn't know, both movies are about crazy women.*

I stared out the window, still crying. It was dark and cloudy outside, those big, thick, gray things about to any second start shedding what made them so heavy-looking in the first place. It was a dreary sight.

I tried to control myself. The last thing I wanted was to just sit there and weep and weep, to be this unappealing, annoying crybaby. I wanted to be like I was before, happy, lively, joking around about everything. But there was nothing I could do to make this new me stop. This was what I had become. And the worst part of it was that, when push came to shove, the why no longer mattered.

I knew Jake wished he could just open the passenger door and throw me out of his car, get rid of this awful person beside him. But he would never do that. Because he still remembered the good times, what I was like before. And he knew, maybe even more than I did, that this new persona was just a temporary one, a temporary monster that would go away some day.

21

MY KNIGHT IN SHINING ARMOR

It took a while before Ruth and I spoke again after that night when she told me that what I was experiencing had nothing to with the many egg donations I had gone through but everything with how life treated me and how I coped with it.

In the weeks that followed, it soon became clear to me that she didn't want to have any part of what was going on since – she started to avoid me. When I called her office, her secretary claimed that she was either busy or not there. Never mind that I once or twice heard Ruth talking in the background. She didn't return any of my calls. I called her up at her home phone, a number that she had given me for emergencies like these. Nobody ever picked up the phone. So I left message after message on the answering machine. Eventually I got the hint.

Naturally, I wasn't happy about the way Ruth had chosen to deal with the situation, but it didn't make me feel as bad as I had thought it would when that night was over. The real rough part had been the minutes following the phone call in which she had claimed she *knew* it was all in my head, since I myself had confided in her not too long ago that I was a pretty unhappy person and that I increasingly felt my life had become meaningless. I think this blow below the belt had been the hardest part to deal with. But the next morning when I woke up, the horror and desolation I had experienced at her cheap action, those intense feelings that had later metamorphosed into anger and frustration, had been exchanged for apathy. I no longer cared about Ruth, whether she was dead or alive, if she was happy or sad, what she thought about me or all of this, whether I would ever see or speak to her again. As a matter of fact, I *hoped* that I would never have to speak to or see her again. The problem was that, in my depressed mind, I had become convinced that as much as I had once considered Ruth the person best equipped to help me into the world of infertility, she had now become the one who could best help me *out* of it. The only thing that mattered to me was how I could get undepressed. And, as I knew my feelings had to do with something chemical in my body – or, more specifically, with my hormones, most likely a lack of estrogen – I was sure that if I only got some estrogen pills, I would feel good once more. Like a junkie needing his smack, I *had* to have my estrogen. I knew that Ruth had easy access to the hormone in all its shapes and forms. Therefore, despite not really wanting to talk to her again, I had kept hounding her until I realized that what I was doing was useless. She would never call me back anyway.

Or at least not until about a month and a half later.

I'm not sure what it was that instigated this change of heart of hers, but one afternoon in the middle of December she did call me back at last.

As she spoke, her voice was filled with remorse.

"How are you doin', sweetie? Any better?"

It took a few seconds before I got over the initial shock of hearing her voice again. But as I did, still being miserable, I concluded it was best not to give in to my first instinct, which had been to slam down the phone in her ear. No, I should take advantage of this sudden opportunity. One way or another I would get some estrogen out of her.

"Maybe a little, I'm not sure, it's hard to tell," I said. "Some days are better than others. But it's still pretty bad." If she said anything about me finding myself a good therapist again, I would definitely hang up on her, though. She didn't.

"I was thinking that maybe you were right, maybe you're feeling like you do mostly because of the hormones. Because of estrogen depletion."

Duuh.

"Well, in that case," she continued, "maybe you'd feel better if you started wearing estrogen patches. I have some here in my office. If you'd like, you can come and pick them up."

Bingo.

Ten minutes later, I sat in my car, on my way over to Ruth's house.

Like previously mentioned, a month and a half had passed since the day we spoke the last time. Since then, I had done little to help myself, despite my friends' repeated pushing and pleading. See, the treacherous thing about being as deeply depressed as I was at that point was the feeling that followed in between the more intense stages, that feeling that everything is meaningless. You are no longer in physical pain exactly; you just truly believe that life sucks. When you feel like that, the last thing on earth you want to do is go through the phone book in search of a psychologist or psychiatrist that maybe, just maybe, sometime in the unforeseeable future, could help make you feel better, feel like there was something to live for. Especially when you *knew* that the only true solution was to get some estrogen in your system. If you only had that, you would get undepressed fast, easily, and efficiently. *Guaranteed.* That was why those quiet periods were almost worse, dangerous even. In those moments I didn't know whether my hormones were still raging or whether this was just the way I normally felt. At least when a headache blasted with full force inside my skull or tears were pouring from my eyes, at least then I knew something was utterly and entirely *wrong* with me, I knew I had to do something to make it go away finally. I *knew* this wasn't me, what I was all about. I could *feel* it. Unfortunately, during those phases I couldn't make any coherent statement or stop crying, and I was definitely not capable of driving over to a doctor to whom I could explain my problems. In short, my situation became a catch-22.

The only time I experienced relief, real relief from this depression was when my period arrived. I didn't even have to check to verify that it indeed had arrived; I could feel it. It was as though the bad feelings within me disappeared at the same time as the blood left my body. That incident further endorsed my conviction that my hormones weren't like they should be.

At any rate, in order to get hold of some estrogen finally, I was willing to drive cross country, which was fortunate since Ruth's house was located more than one and a half hours from where I lived. I had to drive over there to pick up what I thought would be the end to my misery.

When I arrived and rang the doorbell Ruth's assistant greeted me. According to her, Ruth wasn't around; this was information I could care less about as long as I got my drugs. In addition to the patches, the girl handed me some birth control pills that she said I should take in case the patches didn't help. Ruth had assured her that these pills were of the good kind, the kind with little progesterone that wouldn't upset me; instead, they would regulate my hormones. For sure.

I started with the patches. They neither improved nor worsened my emotional state. So I began taking the pills. It would turn out that these pills would do just the opposite of what Ruth had promised they would; they would prolong my depression and intensify it.

On the third or fourth day this became painfully clear to me as I noticed a rapid deterioration and was overcome with fierce attacks of renewed power. I soon threw them out, together with every other birth control pack nurses and doctors and Ruth had given me over the years that I for some inexplicable reason had saved.

And with that, I was back to square one.

◆◆◆

It was the beginning of January already when I finally made myself drive over to that tall black building located about ten minutes by car from where I lived. In this building, on the ninth floor he sat, the person that validated me and what I had known all along. He was a man in his late fifties maybe, short and a little on the heavy side, balding. His nose seemed a bit too long and wide for his small face. The large ears stuck out from his head, making him look like he, in some absurd way, could be related to Dumbo. I didn't think that he was ever what most people would consider a handsome man, but to me he was the most beautiful person on earth. He was my knight in shining armor, my prince on a white horse. My savior. To him there was no question what my problem was: I was suffering from a severe hormone imbalance.

"Right now, the best thing for you to do is to wait it out. You'll see that in a few months all this will be behind you." His voice, when he spoke, was like the one I imagined Santa Claus possessed: warm, deep, kind. "I can't believe this woman told you to take birth control pills. Adding any more hormones to somebody in your state is like adding gasoline to a bonfire instead of water when you want to extinguish it – it's only going to make things worse."

I had just spent an hour reciting my life as an egg donor up until now for Dr. Weinberg. He had been listening patiently. When I was done he told me that it wasn't even necessary for me to go through any tests unless I really wanted to; they would just rack up my fees, as I didn't have insurance. He assured me that there was nothing dangerous about my state, and then he explained once more that, unfortunately, there was really nothing that could be done about it but wait until my body regulated itself naturally. It shouldn't take too long. He did recognize that I must be in tremendous pain emotionally, however, so he wrote me a prescription for Serafem – a type of Prozac especially designed for women with Premenstrual Dysphoric Disorder, which was the fancy clinical name for extreme PMS. He made it so that it would be good for six months. He told me that, by then, I should be fine.

Dr. Jeremiah Weinberg, one of Los Angeles's most reputable gynecologists, had been recommended to me by one of my clients. As time had gone by, it had become harder and harder for me to hide my depression while training. Complaining about broken contacts only worked for so long. One day Rita, my client and a nurse by profession, asked me if everything was OK with me; lately, it hadn't seemed like it. It didn't take long before her probing had poked a hole in the thick emotional shield I had been forced to develop to continue training my clients and I began to cry, sobbingly confessing what I had been going through in the recent months. As it happened, Rita was not only a mature and understanding person when it came to these kinds of embarrassing tell-alls, a person that didn't find you pathetic and despicable a week after for showing such weakness, she also knew exactly the right individual for me to speak to regarding the matter. The next day she had made an appointment for me. And that was how I ended up in Dr. Weinberg's office.

After two weeks on Serafem, that thick layer of despair and negativity that I had gotten so used to wearing had shed almost entirely. I began working out and eating right once more, I worried about how I looked, and I made plans for the future. I stopped smoking, an ancient habit that I had picked up anew. It was OK to wake up in the mornings. I could read and write and concentrate without any problems. Going to the movies was fun again; being a personal trainer wasn't all that bad; I was no longer completely alone in the world. Everybody didn't hate me. Maybe I would indeed publish my novel one day. No, not maybe, I *would* publish it. Fairly soon.

About three weeks later it was as if the last few months had never happened. It was as though I had just dreamed it all. Had I really been feeling *that* bad? It seemed so unreal to me now. But I knew that that was part of it, the deceptive, scary part, that, when it is behind you, you feel like you just imagined everything.

When June rolled around, four months later, I stopped taking antidepressants; I figured that, by now, I had to be back to normal. It turned out that I was. Once in a while though, I was experiencing – surprise, surprise – *PMS* before my periods; at times, fairly intensely and prolonged, up until a week sometimes. Miniature versions of what had once taken place. Eventually they too vanished.

It is now over three years ago since that last donation. Nowadays I live in New York City instead Los Angeles and I really do like it. It is more my kind of town. I have spoken to Ruth on a couple of occasions, although to say that we are friends would be an exaggeration.

Needless to say, despite not being exactly rich yet, I no longer donate – sell – my eggs, even someone who likes to play with fire as much as I do have my limits. No, there are other, safer ways to make a living. Like, for example, the other day when I was reading the *New York Times* I saw this ad. In it, they were looking for kidney donors. Did you know that you can make *50,000 dollars* doing that and... (Just kidding!)

EPILOGUE

As I look back at my years as a multiple donor now, I realize that I should be very happy that a hormone imbalance making me finally experience PMS – with a vengeance! – was all I acquired. (I actually do experience PMS every now and then still, by the way; however, not on a regular basis). I could have had a heart attack, ended up infertile or in a coma, maybe even died. No amount of money in the world is worth gambling with your health. I think this notion has finally entered my mind. I'm not immortal, neither am I Superwoman, hard as it is accepting these truths. These days I make my living waiting tables instead while trying to make it in the world of publishing. I don't have nearly as much money as I used to and I have to admit that sometimes it is a drag to go to work, but one thing is for sure – I have never felt better.

ACKNOWLEDGEMENTS

I want to profusely thank the following people for helping me make this book a reality: Johanna Landberg, Evelyn Encarnacion, Lisa Walter, Lynnae Savage, Arlene O'Connor, Nira Burstein, Seth Duncan, Doug Devita, Kristen Forkeutis, Yvette Avenhall, and Eric Poholsky. Everyone of you provided crucial assistance.

Give the Gift of *Confessions of a Serial Egg Donor* to Your Friends and Colleagues.
Check Your Local Book Store or Order Here

YES, I want ___ copies of *Confessions of a Serial Egg Donor* for $13.95 each. Include $3.95 shipping and handling for one book, and $1.95 for each additional book. Colorado, Ohio, and New York residents must include applicable sales tax. Canadian orders must include payment in US funds, with 7% GST added.

Payment must accompany orders. Allow 2 weeks for delivery.

My check or money order for $_____is enclosed.
Please charge my __ Visa __MasterCard __ American Express

Name _____

Organization _____

Address _____

City/State/Zip_____

Phone _____ E-mail _____

Card # _____

Exp. Date _____ Signature _____

Call (646) 425-9000
Make your checks payable and return to
Adrenaline Books
Park West Finance Station
P.O. Box 20192
New York, NY 10025
www.adrenalinebooks.com